All For Jesus Series

SAM POLLARD
OF
YUNNAN

BY
ERNEST H. HAYES

Author of
"The Concise Guides," "Yarns on Social Pioneers,"
etc., etc.

*"Swift to the head of the army.
Swift spring to your places,
Pioneers! O, Pioneers!"*

Schmul Publishers
Rare Reprint Specialists
Salem, Ohio 44460
1978

Printed by
Old Paths Tract Society, Inc.
Shoals, Indiana 47581

PREFACE

HERE is an epic story that reads like a romance and has thrilling episodes that remind us of the gallant exploits of David Livingstone, the prince of missionary pioneers.

Sam Pollard was one of those rare souls of whom it could be truly said " he reminds us of Jesus Christ." His story of achievement, adventure and sacrifice in remote parts of unknown China deserves to be widely known, for it will fertilise the imagination of youth, quicken the pulse, and stimulate enthusiasm for Christian service of a type much needed to-day.

My thanks are due to Pollard's widow, and to his colleague and successor, Rev. W. H. Hudspeth, for encouragement and help in this labour of love, and for reading the manuscript. I am also indebted to W. A. Grist's biography, " Samuel Pollard, Pioneer Missionary in China " and to Pollard's own little books, " Tight Corners in China " and " The Story of the Miao," to which the reader is referred for more detailed treatment.

One hopes that Mrs. Pollard's moving appeal at the end of this book will win a response worthy the need and opportunity.

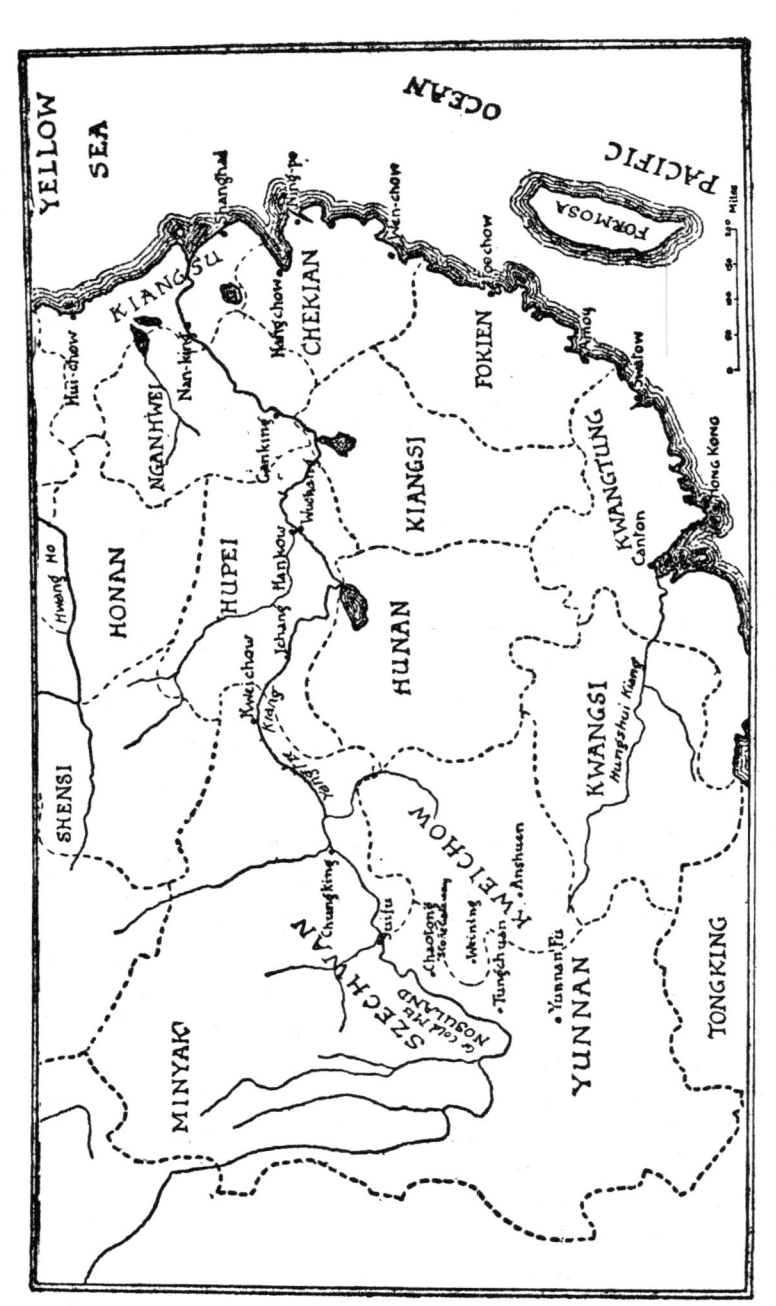

MAP ILLUSTRATING POLLARD'S WORK.

CONTENTS

AND DATED SUMMARY OF THE LIFE OF SAM POLLARD

DATE.	CHAPTER.	PAGE

I. EASTWARD HO!   7

1864	Pollard born at Camelford, Cornwall	8
1886	Volunteers for pioneer work in Yunnan	13
1887	Sails from London for China	13
,,	Arrives at Shanghai (March)	14

II. A NARROW ESCAPE FROM THE TIGER   16

1887	Learning the language at Ganking (March)	16
,,	Starts on the *Yangtze* for Yunnan (November)	20
,,	Nearly drowned in the Ch'in T'an Rapids	23

III. SETTLING IN AT CHAOTONG   26

1888	Overland through Szechwan and Yunnan (Jan.)	26
,,	Reaches Chaotong and starts work (February)	27
,,	Nurses Dymond through smallpox (March)	30
,,	Sets out for Yunnan Fu (June)	36

IV. PIONEERING WITH GONG AND CORNET   37

1888	First preaching work in the capital (June)	39
1889	On tour with gong and Bible	41
1891	Is married to Emma Hainge (December)	47
1892	Attracting the crowds by cornet	48

V. RELIEVING FAMINE AND FACING RIOT   50

1892	Floods spread devastation round Yunnan	51
1893	Mission station built in Yunnan Fu	53
1895	Furlough in England	55
1897	Resumes work at Chaotong (April)	55
1899	Stabbing affray in mission courtyard (May)	60
1900	Boxer storm bursts—Pollard forced back to Shanghai	62

Contents

DATE.	CHAPTER.	PAGE
	VI. BACK IN YUNNAN	63
1901	Work resumed at Chaotong (February)	63
1902	Extensive tours through Yunnan begun	65
1903	First contacts with Nosu Chiefs	68

	VII. ENTERING THE FORBIDDEN LAND	71
1903	Visit to Nosu chiefs on Great Cold Mountains	73
,,	The dilemma of an offer of marriage	79
1904	Narrow escape from attack at the ferry	81

	VIII. THE COMING OF THE SCOUTS	84
1904	Four Miao visit the Chaotong Mission (July)	84
,,	More Miao visitors arrive	87
,,	The great Miao swarm	89

	IX. CHAMPION OF THE OPPRESSED	92
1904	Outbreak of persecution against Pollard	93
1905	First preaching journey among the Miao	94
,,	Pollard set apart for work among the Miao	99

	X. WITHIN AN INCH OF DEATH	101
1905	Founding of the Stone Gateway Mission	101
,,	First baptisms of hundreds of Miao (November)	105
,,	Mass movement of Miao towards Christianity	106
1906	Opening of out-stations on the hills	107
1907	Almost beaten to death at Ha-lee-mee	111

	XI. THE WORD OF THE LORD	115
1908	Second furlough in England	116
1910	Resumes work among Miao at Stone Gateway	117
1911	Training college opened for native teachers	117
,,	Invents Miao alphabet and translates Scriptures	118
1912	The revolution—Pollard at Yunnan Fu (Jan.)	120
,,	Starts work again at Stone Gateway (April)	121
1915	The Great War and its reaction in Yunnan	122
,,	Death of Pollard at Stone Gateway (September)	126

SAM POLLARD OF YUNNAN

Chapter One — EASTWARD HO!

"LOOK out! Here comes Tommy!" The loud whisper worked a marvellous change in the big dormitory of Shebbear Grammar School. A game of "footer" with a tennis ball, that had been in progress between the beds down the long room, stopped abruptly. Two boys who were mending a fishing rod tossed the thing under the nearest bed. Others, who had been doing anything but undress, now began to remove their outer garments with feverish haste.

A second later, Thomas Ruddle, the headmaster, put his head through the doorway, gave a searching glance round the room, and with a gruff "Good-night, boys," departed.

Thanks to the warning of the boy who, being a newcomer, had the bed nearest the door, the visit of "Tommy" passed off without regrettable consequences, and after some further larks the boys got into bed. Almost the last to turn in was Sam Pollard, who produced a dog-eared Bible from a drawer where it had rested cheek by jowl with an old dictionary, an out-of-date time-table, a magnifying glass,

Sam Pollard of Yunnan

and a number of odds and ends of no value to anyone but their schoolboy owner.

As Sam crossed the dormitory to read his " daily portion " by the light of the smoky lantern which cast a feeble circle of yellow light on some of the bare boards below, he was nearly tripped up by a mischievous room-mate who stuck out a leg at the critical moment. Sam was Christian enough to be true to his promise to read the Bible daily, but not to the extent of forgiving such an offence. Tossing his Bible on his bed, he pummelled the offender till the boy yelled for mercy, then quietly picked up the book and fulfilled his promise to his father.

Samuel Pollard, senior, was the Bible Christian minister at Penryn, Cornwall, and by dint of great self-sacrifice had sent young Sam when twelve years old to finish his education at Shebbear in North Devon, the denominational boarding school. Sam, who was born on April 20th, 1864 during his father's ministry at Camelford, Cornwall, had been subject to a powerful, but sane and sweet, religious influence from his earliest days. Small in stature, with a massive forehead and big, thoughtful eyes, the boy possessed a distinctive personality. People who judged from his appearance that he was slow and flabby, quickly found out their mistake when anything occurred to ruffle Sam's normal amiability. Fire would then flash from those big eyes, and his placid face would glow with animation. In pranks he could outmatch most of the mischievous

Eastward Ho!

youngsters in the school, and hold his own in repartee with boys much older than himself. But the slightest suggestion of nastiness would call forth such stinging rebuke and biting invective as would not easily be forgotten by the offender.

Towards the end of his schooldays Sam won first-class honours in the Oxford Locals, and at a Civil Service Examination came out sixth in the whole country. This success elated him greatly, for it secured him a position in the Post Office Savings Bank in London, with an initial salary that was bigger than his father would ever receive as a minister.

With high hopes, therefore, Sam—a somewhat shy youth of seventeen—came to London to make a career for himself. His letters home were full of the scenes and events of the great metropolis, but his parents at Penryn had few fears for his welfare, for soon after his eleventh birthday Sam had dedicated his life to the service of Jesus Christ, and "knew Whom he had believed." From the beginning of his life in London, the youth found a welcome at the Bible Christian chapel at Clapham, where for six years he remained under the influence of F. W. Bourne, a minister of unusual gifts and spiritual power.

As a result of both his home training and his minister's influence, Sam reached man's estate with bigger plans for his life than could be satisfied by the Civil Service. The idea that he might follow in his father's footsteps had been mooted before this. In a letter

Sam Pollard of Yunnan

home during the summer of 1886, Sam, who is concerned over throat trouble, writes:
"I can't understand how I am to be a minister if I am to have a chronic bad throat; and I am under the impression that God has distinctly called me to work for Him in this way. Perhaps you remember that some time ago I did not look at all favourably on the possibility of being a minister; nothing seemed further from my ideas. Yet now I have been brought to such a state that I would rather be a B.C. (Bible Christian) minister than anything else in the world. It seems like a very passion with me at times, and I hardly dare contemplate the idea of not being able to preach for Christ."

From that position it was a natural step for Sam to look beyond the borders of his native land for a sphere of service. Once again we find evidence of the power of David Livingstone — that prince of missionary heroes — to fertilise the imagination of young men and win them for Christian service abroad. From his youth Sam Pollard had been familiar with the discoveries and soaring ambitions of Livingstone in Africa, and doubtless the example of that indomitable pioneer now fired him to seek work overseas. The Bible Christians, merged with two other denominations into the United Methodist Church since 1907, had been a missionary Church from their inception, and at this particular time were on the threshold of a great development abroad.

Only a few months before Sam wrote to his father about entering the ministry, one of his

Eastward Ho!

friends, Samuel Thorne, together with Thomas Vanstone, had been set apart by their Church for pioneer work in Yunnan, in the southwest corner of China. The Bible Christians had been confining their overseas activities to Canada, Australia and New Zealand, but now the United Church caught the vision of taking part in the tremendous work of evangelising the great Chinese Empire. The province of Yunnan was chosen, after consultation with the China Inland Mission, as being one of the largest and most needy of the unoccupied mission fields. The annual conference of the denomination, held at Bideford that year, had caught fire when the Yunnan project was outlined, and seven hundred pounds were promised in a few minutes for an immediate start. Thorne and Vanstone were there and then valedicted for Yunnan with great enthusiasm.

It is not strange, therefore, that young Sam Pollard was caught in this tornado of missionary ardour. From that time forward the dominating purpose of his life was to claim a share in annexing Yunnan for the Kingdom of God. With prophetic certainty he added a sentence to a letter to his parents at that time that fell like a bombshell into the manse at Penryn :

" Vanstone and Thorne have just left for China, and I shall be the next."

His mother's heart sank like lead when she read those words, for she recoiled from the sacrifice involved in giving her son to China. Neither of the parents knew what to say in

Sam Pollard of Yunnan

reply to Sam's letter, so for some time the subject was not mentioned. Meanwhile Sam went about his Post Office work in London with a fixed determination that a different vocation was before him. The vision he had seen of China's uncounted millions waiting for Christ was inescapable. Patiently he set to work to win his parents' consent, but for a long time his mother held out against the project.

The end of that fateful year found Sam Pollard on his knees at the watch-night service of his church at Clapham. The few remaining minutes of the old year were passing. Men and women were using the fleeting moments for thanksgiving and confession, for re-dedication and fuller surrender. Under stress of the emotion of the situation Sam begged his fellow-worshippers to pray that his mother might give her consent for him to go to China, and that other difficulties might be removed.

At the same tense moment, three hundred miles from Clapham, Samuel Pollard, senior, was conducting a watch-night service at St. Just, Cornwall. In one of the front pews sat the preacher's wife in an agony of prayer. As the chapel clock struck the hour of midnight and so ushered in the New Year, the struggle between mother-love and a sense of the will of God reached its climax. In the eloquent silence that followed the midnight chime a woman's voice was heard saying faintly:

" Yes, Lord, you shall have him."

Eastward Ho!

Prayer in London had been answered at St. Just! Following a talk with his mother soon afterwards, the son offered himself for missionary work, and was at once accepted. Thereupon he resigned an assured position for life in the Civil Service for the perilous insecurity of pioneer missionary work, not merely without a pang of regret, but in the gay abandon of a knight setting out on the quest.

"One glowing heart sets another afire." When Sam volunteered for China, his action brought another Shebbear boy, Frank Dymond, to the same position. In those early days the need for action was so urgent, and the spirit of the whole Church so quickened, that little time could be spared for special training. Sam and Frank were accepted by the Committee, dedicated for their work at the Southsea Conference of 1886, and early in the following year sailed from London for the Far East.

At long last Sam and his friend had their first glimpse of the shores of China. They bade farewell to the officers of their ship at Woosung, and started by tug to Shanghai. Eagerly they looked for their first contact with the yellow waters of the mighty Yangtze-Kiang, for the famous "Yellow Tiger" had been much in their conversation for days. Soon their tug threaded its way through a thickly-spread fleet of the queerest craft that Pollard had ever seen—picturesque Chinese junks of all sizes and conditions, carrying odd-shaped

Sam Pollard of Yunnan

sails that seemed quite out of proportion to the craft that carried them.

Pollard's quick imagination was busy as he watched the never-ending procession of junks that met them as they made for Shanghai. Before him was the mouth of the great riverway that twisted and turned for thousands of miles into the very heart of unknown China. He felt that for weal or woe his future was bound up with the sullen yellow stream that emptied itself so placidly into the sea. He had been warned that in going up the Yangtze he was literally putting himself into the tiger's mouth. All too soon he was to know how sharp were its teeth, but for the present he laughed gaily with his friend at the ludicrous side of Chinese river-life that unrolled itself before their eyes.

When the two recruits stepped ashore at Shanghai they could not complain of lack of welcome. They were met by three missionaries of the C.I.M., and entertained on the following day by Dr. Muirhead of the London Missionary Society. In company with these new friends they explored the city, and were greatly impressed by the splendour of the buildings of the foreign concessionaires.

More interesting to Pollard, however, was his first glimpse of the native city, with its teeming population and congested medley of life thronging around him.

"What is one among so many?" he said to himself again and again. An ordinary man might have quailed at the mere thought of the

Eastward Ho!

purpose that had brought him from the West. How could one stranger expect to make any impression upon a vast continent, with a population as countless as the grains of sand on a seashore? But Sam Pollard "knew Whom he had believed," and braced himself for his task with a courage and a gaiety that marked him out as a true knight of the cross.

A Chinese Wayside Shrine.

Chapter
Two

A NARROW ESCAPE
FROM THE TIGER

"YOU look like the real thing now, Frank," said Pollard with a grin, as he carefully inspected his companion.

"And so do you, Sam," Dymond retorted; "don't you wish you could get into the language as easily?"

The two friends were chaffing each other over their changed appearance. A tailor and a barber had completely transformed the missionaries. In their long quilted coats, black skull-caps, and flowing pigtails, temporarily artificial, they looked like Chinese. When they opened their lips, however, their humiliating lack of the one thing needful was immediately shown.

Pollard determined to lose no time in grappling with the difficult task of mastering the language. A further journey of three days up the Yellow Tiger—the Yangtze—took them to Ganking, where the C.I.M. had established a Training Home for missionaries. There, under Principal Baller, Pollard began the study of the thousands of Chinese characters, with their subtle variations in pronunciation which make the classical Chinese language almost beyond knowledge for ordinary people. Sam soon outstripped Frank Dymond and almost every other student by his progress, not only

A Narrow Escape from the Tiger

in mastering the language, but in gaining a knowledge of the Chinese classics. His characteristic energy and enthusiasm made him stick closely to his studies, encouraged by the Principal, who recognised his promise. Such was Sam's progress that three months after reaching the Training Home, he was asked to take evening prayers in Chinese on alternate nights. At first he shrank from the ordeal, as there would be a number of Chinese present, but on second thoughts determined to justify his principal's confidence.

"You can imagine how I trembled," he says in a letter to his mother, "though there were only a few present. We read together the story of the woman touching the hem of Christ's garment: then I tried to say a few words on the subject. They said they understood me, but so polite are they that you could never find a Chinese who would tell you otherwise. I felt happy after it was over, walking up the garden. It was only a little done, but it was a little for the Master, and that cheered my heart. The road to the heart of this language is long—very long; but even the longest roads are pleasant when walking in company with Him."

Two months later the students sat for their first examination, and Pollard waited anxiously for the results. When these were posted up he was surprised and elated to find his name at the head of the list, with 392 marks out of a possible 400. The students had a holiday for the rest of the day, to celebrate the occasion,

Sam Pollard of Yunnan

and Sam took the lead in the fun and laughter, but that night his elation was moderated by a growing concern about his spiritual life. So much attention to study and the mental equipment for his work had inevitably reacted on his spiritual state. The next night he remained on his knees long after the other men had gone to bed, determined not to move until he had got the blessing he sought. God answered his challenge, and the following evening, after the Sunday services, he led the way to the top of the house and conducted a students' prayer meeting of no ordinary kind. We give Pollard's own account to his father of what happened, because it reveals the secret of his remarkable life-work afterwards.

"It was warm, and as we were in for a struggle we took off our gowns and knelt down. Oh, Dad, it would have done your heart good to have been there. What was the result? A mighty blessing, like to shake the house. Some of us got very happy, and the scene that followed was just like some of our Pensilva or Penryn revivals. I was about the noisiest! By simple faith we laid hold of the power held out to us. I told the Lord how often we had, when pointing sinners to Him, told them just to believe and lay hold of the blessing, and now we desired to take our own prescription. I shall never forget that moment. Bless God, the power came immediately, and to-day, after more than a fortnight, I am a different fellow. We appear to have alarmed the natives in the surrounding houses that night. They came

A Narrow Escape from the Tiger

on Monday morning to enquire who was dead in the house. With them a death always occasions a lot of shouting and crying. They were quite right; several of us died that night, and the life we now live, we live by faith in the Son of God."

This Pentecostal experience in the upper room was not allowed to pass off in mere effervescence. Next day those students began preaching in Chinese in the hall attached to the Training Home. Dymond and the others preached to all who cared to come and listen, but Pollard, characteristically, was not satisfied with that. Borrowing Dymond's concertina, on which he could not play a single tune, he proceeded to pull the instrument in and out, making a great deal of noise, even if there were no music.

This had the desired effect. The unearthly din brought a crowd of curious Chinese to the door. What they expected to see is not on record, although Sam himself suggests a wild-beast show. Having invited the people to come in and sit down, he sang a few hymns to them. Then having learned that the Chinese put high value on filial piety, Pollard told them how his father in England had told him again and again of Christ's love, until at last he had been converted. Then he went on to declare, "there is not a better man than my father" thus putting himself at one with his audience, who prided themselves on being good sons. The experiment proved very satisfactory, for quite a number of Chinese

Sam Pollard of Yunnan

heard the old, old story that afternoon, and seemed impressed by it.

At the final language examination Sam and Frank came through with flying colours, and by the middle of November they prepared to depart for Chaotong, an important city in the province of Yunnan, which was to be the scene of their maiden efforts as missionaries. Fortunately they were to travel up the river with Thomas Vanstone, who had been down to Shanghai to be married. The Vanstones reached Ganking on the " Kwang Fu ", a Chinese river-steamer, and the two young men joined them on the boat. Sam found great delight in mixing with the Chinese passengers perfectly tongue-free, able to converse with strangers in an intelligent manner. They reached Hankow two days later, and then bade farewell to the " Kwang Fu ".

Their thoughts were now set on the great province of Yunnan, and the long journey by water that faced them. After seemingly endless bargaining, Vanstone hired a native houseboat and crew for the next stage of their journey to Sha-si. This would take at least a fortnight, and after all preparations had been made, they started up-river. The boat was very comfortable, and consisted of four rooms. The room in the bow, being the largest, was used by the missionary party as dining room, chapel and study combined. Behind this were two smaller rooms, one the sleeping apartment of the Vanstones, and the other the cabin of Pollard and Dymond. The room in the stern

A Narrow Escape from the Tiger

was occupied by the Chinese crew. As the boat only travelled at about twenty miles a day, it was quite easy for the missionaries to get out for a walk or a scramble over the rocks whenever they wanted to stretch their legs.

Day succeeded day, in this pleasant way, each bringing fresh scenery. The quiet-moving waters of the broad river seemed to contradict the stories that Sam had heard about the mighty Yangtze, which cuts China in two from west to east. It seemed hard to believe that those who knew the river best called it a raging, fierce, unmanageable tiger. Up to that point the few rapids and eddies they had passed seemed nothing more than the playful, good-natured teasing of a kitten. Then slowly but surely the scene changed, and before long Sam had a full taste of the tiger's rage, that bit into his memory so deeply that he could never afterwards hear or speak of the Yangtze without a quickening of the heart-beat. He must be allowed to tell the story in his own vivid way.

· · · ·

Soon after we had travelled a thousand miles up the Yangtze we noticed the waters getting swifter and the shores more rugged, and we eagerly looked out for the rapids. Soon we passed over a few of the small rapids, and enjoyed the rush of the waters immensely. The men on the shore, who were pulling us up-stream by long bamboo ropes, did not like the extra work the rapids brought, but we

Sam Pollard of Yunnan

who sat and watched enjoyed the extra excitement. At last, on December 13th, we reached the famous Ch'in T'an Rapid, one of the two greatest rapids which boats at that time went over.

In our front-room we had chairs and a table; and several boxes acted as a sideboard and a bookcase. Right over the table there hung —not a lamp or a gas bracket, or a pot of maidenhair fern (though that fern abounds)— no! nothing like that, but something much better and more interesting. There hung from the roof a real Christmas pudding, all tempting, and stirring up memories of home and friends. The lady of our party had made the pudding early, so that it might last all the longer— we looked at it, and then let our eyes stray to the calendar on the wall, to see how many days were left to the 25th!

We decorated the walls with photographs, and one pigtail—a coloured one—was hanging from a nail. Sometimes the pigtails got tired of us, or rather we of them, and then we gave ourselves a rest by hanging them on the wall. Our study books, Bibles, hymn-books, field-glasses, rugs and all kinds of odds and ends were lying about. Frank Dymond was sitting at the head of the boat watching the men working at the ropes on the shore. The rest of us were chatting away in the front-room, with the door shut because of the mid-winter cold.

The great river had treated us so well that we had got to like it and to think it was always

A Narrow Escape from the Tiger

kind. Suddenly there was a great shout and a rush to the front of the boat by the few men left on board.

What is it? The boat is heeling over toward the left! It is very difficult to keep our footing! We rush to the right to help to press down the boat on that side. How the river must have laughed as we did this, for in a moment it came pouring into our room, overwhelming everything. Then we knew we were wrecked in the great Ch'in T'an Rapid, and were to be tossed and torn by the fierce, angry, boiling waters.

I tried all I could to creep along, inch by inch, towards the door, but the roaring waters smote me down, trampled on me, and in a few minutes our boat and all on board were covered by the waters of the Yangtze. We could neither get forward, backward, nor upward! In our hearts, however, there was hope and no fear. "God has called us to be His missionaries in West China, and He won't let us be drowned here," was our thought.

Then came a change. The fierce, angry Tiger River got its teeth into our boat and tore it like matchwood, tossing boards, mats, oars, masts, and sails in all directions. Thus we found a way up to the surface, and in the whirling backwaters, clinging to bits of wreckage. There were Mr. and Mrs. Vanstone, hand in hand, looking very wet, but keeping up their spirits and clinging to a wooden box. Frank Dymond was nowhere to be seen!

What was the end to be? It was most

Sam Pollard of Yunnan

difficult to swim in those terrible waters, and our long, wadded Chinese gowns sucked us down terribly. But terrible as the fierce river was, there was One more powerful, and though we did not see Him walk on the waters towards us, we knew He was there. Men on the shore were shouting excitedly, " The Red Boat! The Red Boat! " And soon two Red Boats were putting off towards the scene of the disaster.

The Chinese lifeboats are painted red, and the Yangtze Red Boat Service is one of the finest services to be found in all China. How eagerly those men rowed! How they beat back the waters! They had fought the Tiger so long, that they had learned how to conquer and almost to despise it. Here they come! How welcome those strong Chinese boatmen! As we were in Chinese dress they thought they were about to save their own countrymen. Coming close up to us they saw the white skin of our faces, and knew we were foreigners. Then they burst out laughing! What!

Are they going to leave the foreigners alone and to laugh as they watch them die? Oh no! Those men had no such thoughts, and before long we were safely on the lifeboats, Mr. and Mrs. Vanstone on one, and I on another. My long wadded gown acted like a sucker, and several men had to pull hard before they got me safely over the side of the boat. It was a tug-of-war between the Tiger River and the expert men, and the men won.

• • • •

A Narrow Escape from the Tiger

Minus hats and pigtails, with their long quilted coats streaming with water, Pollard and the Vanstones were safely landed on the muddy banks of the Yangtze, looking like scarecrows. A crowd of gaping natives seemed to spring up from nowhere, and to regard the foreigners' plight as a huge joke. To Pollard's immense relief Frank Dymond was brought to shore in another Red Boat a few minutes later. The shipwrecked foreigners were taken to an inn and treated with much kindness by the people of Ch'in T'an. Every effort was made to salvage their belongings, but it was found afterwards that nineteen of their boxes—and the Christmas pudding—had been devoured by the ferocious Tiger.

Next day the party were able to hire two small boats, by which they reached Kuei Fu, and from that city they travelled by another boat to Chungking, a voyage which lasted a fortnight. Pollard described the captain of this boat as the queerest specimen of a Chinaman he had ever seen, while the crew were a ragamuffin, deplorable set. He was profoundly thankful when they reached Chungking in safety, for the gross incompetency of the captain more than once brought them within an ace of a second disaster.

Pollard said that he reminded him of the Mississippi pilot who boasted that he knew every rock on the river—and as the boat struck while he was speaking, he had the presence of mind to add "And that's one of them!"

Chapter Three SETTLING IN AT CHAOTONG

WITH a sigh of relief Pollard and his friends turned their backs on the Yangtze on the 7th January, 1888. They had covered 1,500 miles at the mercy of the Tiger, and were glad that they could thenceforward take the long trail overland to Yunnan. They soon found, however, that so far as peril was concerned, they were "out of the frying-pan into the fire." The province of Szechwan, through a corner of which they had to travel, had been the scene of anti-foreign riots not many months earlier. It was not deemed safe, therefore, for the four foreigners to travel together.

Pollard and Dymond accordingly separated from the Vanstones and went on, with a pony between them. They took it in turns to ride—an arrangement that apparently did not please the animal, for he gave them a good deal of trouble. He had an unpleasant habit of kneeling down and rolling over in the water whenever their road took them through a stream—which happened very frequently! For a month they jogged along with varying experiences, enduring plenty of hardships. But nothing could depress the high spirits of the wayfarers, and Pollard in particular was as full of glee as a schoolboy on holiday. At last the majestic hills of Yunnan could be seen raising their solid bastions to the

Settling in at Chaotong

distant sky, and beckoning the eager travellers on to their goal.

When Pollard and Dymond at last climbed the hills into Yunnan itself, they were not merely elated by the sense of having reached their promised land after twelve months' journeying from England, but were amazed at the beauty of their surroundings, and thrilled by the perils of the path.

"The scenery," Pollard says, "is indescribably grand; up and down cliffs and over rugged rocks we ride and tramp all day. Once we had to go along a ledge where there was scarcely room to walk. Passing a fine waterfall I stopped and looked: it almost took my breath away. Dare I take the pony across such a path? One false step and we should be hurled down an abyss. A few moments of nerve tension and of desperate resolve, and we were over in safety. On the other side of the river the cliff rose in a sheer mass for a thousand feet."

Exactly one month after leaving the treacherous Yangtze behind, they began their last climb before reaching the extensive plateau—6,000 feet above sea-level—on which stood Chaotong. Entering the north gate of the city on the evening of February 8th, their appearance aroused some curiosity, but heedless of that they hurried through the narrow streets, in search of the little house where Sam Thorne lived. As they were not expected to arrive that day, their sudden appearance proved a joyous surprise. With great delight Thorne

Sam Pollard of Yunnan

ushered them into the poor little Chinese house rented for half-a-crown a month since his arrival a few months earlier.

The meanness of the room in which they sat, dimly lighted by a smoky Chinese candle, troubled them little, nor did the straight-backed, uncomfortable chairs, the coarse food provided for their supper, and the tiny loft upstairs into which Pollard and Dymond eventually climbed for rest. That night the three old Shebbear boys talked into the small hours, reminiscent of the past and optimistic as to the future.

Early next morning Sam was roving round the city, getting his bearings for future work. A man of lesser courage would have been seized with dismay at the wretched, badly-paved, dirty streets of this obscure inland city, where abject poverty was rife. He soon realised that their tiny house was excellently placed, for it was opposite a large Confucian temple, and within a stone's throw of the Examination Hall where every three years students gathered from a wide area to sit for the coveted B.A. degree.

When the Vanstones arrived two days later the house was sadly overcrowded, but none cared about that. Finding that the presence of such a large band of foreigners created quite a stir in the city and brought crowds of people to the doors, each took a turn at preaching at what became an all-day evangelistic meeting. Probably the language of the foreigners betrayed the fact again and again that they were mere learners, and no doubt the curious, gaping

Settling in at Chaotong

crowd understood little of the message delivered, but the gallant efforts made in those hectic first days were never forgotten.

A few days later the little missionary band broke up. The Vanstones went on to Yunnan Fu, Thorne went off to Chungking to get married, and the two recruits were left in charge of the mission. They found themselves alone in a densely-populated city where foreigners were seldom seen, and were therefore objects of curiosity and suspicion.

For Pollard the days that followed were " one continuous grind at language study and evangelism." There was neither time nor opportunity for recreation. Every moment that could be spared was used in mastering new words. Every day they went out to preach at street corners and in open places, taking it in turns to deliver the message and pray for power and blessing. Afterwards they would separate, going through the streets selling Christian tracts and books. Pollard generally finished up by preaching in the central market where the riff-raff of the city gathered—the fortune-tellers, the quack doctors, the gamblers, the story-tellers, and the boys on the look-out for mischief and fun. Under these conditions life was never dull or monotonous. The congregations were constantly on the move, and sometimes a listener began an argument with the missionary that made matters very interesting to the audience. Towards evening the two chums returned home, and after tea came a Chinese service and more study. At last, thoroughly

Sam Pollard of Yunnan

worn out, they would climb the ladder into the loft, " and so to bed."

Then came a terrible ordeal that brought home to Pollard the terrifying isolation of their position, and how near the edge of the abyss they lived at that time. Frank Dymond fell ill. Up in that loft, without direct light or ventilation, he tossed in fever and great pain day after day. What was the malady? That question haunted Pollard's mind every moment of the day. The first urgent need was to diagnose the complaint. Let Pollard take up the narrative now.

.   .   .   .

We had one or two medical books, and these we consulted. I remember so well how I turned over page after page, eagerly reading the descriptions of the symptoms of various diseases. At the best of times such reading is depressing. We were trying to solve a problem that meant much to both of us. Could those terrible headaches and that distressing sickness mean malaria fever, the scourge so dreaded by missionaries? Or did they mean typhoid fever, the slayer of multitudes? Or were they after all, but the signs of acute indigestion which would disappear in a few days?

Page after page I read on, carefully tracing the descriptions of the symptoms. At last I hit on a description which tallied exactly. Line after line agreed minutely. I looked up at the title on the page, and the name of the

Settling in at Chaotong

sickness knocked me all of a heap. No! No!! No!!! It cannot possibly be that! I resolved to try something simpler and more easily nursed, and that did not so frequently end in death, a coffin, and a grave. It seemed as if the fascinating, horrible book was full of diseases, all inviting me to take my choice. But somehow or other I found myself wandering back to that page where Frank's latest photograph seemed all too faithful and lifelike.

At last we were compelled to accept the inevitable. We realised we were in for a great fight with a horrible, relentless foe, who revels in slaughter. The Chinese name for it is "The Flowers of Heaven", for they are afraid to speak of it in terms befitting its relentless, cruel nature, lest the demons who control it should be offended, and take a terrible revenge. Under the attractive name of "The Flowers of Heaven" who would ever dream there dwelt that dreaded and highly-infectious disease of smallpox.

Smallpox! And we were ill-prepared for the struggle. Can you imagine it? In a poor little house at a rent of 7½d. a week! And no doctor nearer than two months! And no nurse at hand! And no proper food! And rough boards to sleep on! And half a paper window in the bedroom! And the roof so low that in parts of the room you could not stand up, while all day long the sun beat pitilessly on the tiles just over the bed, as if it wanted to bake the sick man before he was dead!

Sam Pollard of Yunnan

We shall never forget those days of horror and dread.

After the first shock we set to work to fight the disease. Day by day, in the best way we knew, we measured our strength, patience, and hope with the enemy. Night and day the fight was a close one.

Sunday came round when the disease was at its height. Frank was indeed very ill. I was tired and almost broken-hearted. I had nursed him night and day, never taking off my clothes, and always ready to attend to his wants. He had become very delirious. When out preaching, the children on the streets had often given us a bad time by shouting after us and tormenting us, in the many ways so well known to boys. In his delirium Frank seemed to see these boys crowding round his bed, and he begged me to drive them away. I had to pretend to do so, and it seemed so strange to be driving away a phantom army of imaginary boys. I can laugh now, as I see myself waving my arms and pursuing a crowd of tormentors who did not exist. My gallant attack always succeeded for a while, and brought some little comfort to my sick companion. It was, however, most disconcerting to be suddenly interrupted by a distressed cry:

"Sam! there they are again! Look! please drive them away for me! They are coming again!"

It was not an easy thing to keep smiling in those circumstances. Sunday afternoon came. Frank believed that the end was coming soon,

Settling in at Chaotong

and I did not see what else there was to expect. I was startled by a request of his;

"Do you think, Sam, we can have the Sacrament together once more before I leave you alone?"

Of course, I was ready to agree to anything that would bring any comfort to my sick chum. The arrangements were not long in making. A couple of Chinese cups, a small pot of tea, and a Chinese biscuit were all that were needed. These I brought up the ladder on a small Chinese tray of a bright red colour. We never use wine for our sacrament, but nearly always plain, weak Chinese tea.

I have scarcely had a harder task in my life. Here was my friend and old school-chum dying, and preparing for his entry into the other world where Jesus apparently wanted him. It was almost more than I could stand, and it was with a very heavy heart I took part in that breaking of bread in the upper room. The singing and the praying went fairly well, and then, as usual, a few words were to be spoken about the dying love of our Saviour. I was supposed to be leading the service, and it was my duty to say those few words, but for the life of me they would not come. Every time I tried to start, instead of words coming, up came a great lump into my throat which I could not swallow, which choked everything, and the tears would run down my cheeks, completing my discomfiture.

Then came a sudden change. Frank took the service out of my hands, and gave the

Sam Pollard of Yunnan

address. I shall never forget the great confidence and faith he had that afternoon. There was no unwillingness to go. Suffering acutely, a swollen mass of sores, the old Shebbear boy lifted his heart to God and thanked Jesus over and over again for His great love. I can assure you that Jesus Himself came to us in that little upper room, and we were wonderfully cheered and comforted by His love and presence. Death seemed to lose all its terrors, and instead there came a vision of glory, and of triumphant entrance into the King's presence. In a way undreamed of by the Chinese, Heavenly Flowers bloomed in that chamber of death. When Frank had finished speaking we drank the tea and ate the biscuit, and in our hearts there was begotten a great loyalty to King Jesus.

After that things gradually got better. Slowly but surely the sick missionary crept up out of the valley of the shadow of death, and by and by, to the great joy of us both, he was able to get up and crawl slowly down that ladder. I went first, so that if he slipped he should have something soft to fall on! By that time we were able to laugh again, and to see the humorous side of our troubles.

．　　．　　．　　．

Even during that hand-to-hand fight with death to save his friend, Pollard did his best to serve the Master in Whose Name they had placed themselves in such a predicament. As

Settling in at Chaotong

may be imagined, in such a filthy and overcrowded city, sickness and disease were rife. Sam was not a fully-qualified doctor, yet he had acquired sufficient medical knowledge to deal with many straightforward cases of illness. In addition to disease, the curse of opium-smoking made frightful ravages in human life. One day Pollard was called from his friend's sick-bed to save the life of an opium suicide. Making Frank as comfortable as possible, and pushing the necessary remedies into a bag, he hurried out and was piloted to a broken-down hovel in a distant part of the city.

Solemnly he was ushered into the presence of his first patient. She was a woman of about thirty, stretched on a couch with eyes shut and teeth tightly clenched. Mixing a strong dose of mustard and water for an effective, if violent emetic, Pollard roused the woman and tried to make her take the dose, but she would have none of it. Time after time he tried to force the medicine down her throat with the help of her relatives, but every time she dashed it away. Flushed and exhausted, he was compelled to rest for a while before making another attempt. Next time he succeeded in making her take the dose, her relatives helping by shouting and swearing angrily at her. In the struggle she seized Sam's pigtail with such a grip that he seriously thought of cutting it off, since it was hampering the cure. By a violent effort the pigtail was at last released, and its sacrifice avoided. The

Sam Pollard of Yunnan

medicine proved effective, and on the following day the woman's husband and her father called on Pollard to thank him for saving her life.

This medical success completely established Pollard's reputation in the city as a healer. From that day forward people began to find their way to the half-a-crown-a-month mission house with all sorts of ailments, and poor Sam, with his very slender knowledge of matters medical, was expected to heal them all. Sometimes he had good success, but was wont to declare that this was due to luck rather than skill.

In June relief arrived for the two young pioneers, who left Chaotong for Yunnan Fu, the capital of the province.

Chapter Four

PIONEERING WITH GONG AND CORNET

POLLARD entered into Yunnan Fu with the pioneering spirit strong upon him. With that quickness of perception and sound insight that marked him out from his fellows, he regarded Yunnan Fu as a strategic centre from which a vast province could be conquered for Christ. The very approach to the city encouraged this view. It was situated on a vast plateau, and surrounded by a fine brick wall thirty feet high, pierced by six gates and surmounted by many towers.

As Sam passed beneath the gloomy portals of one of these gates and entered the city, he seemed to have stepped back into an earlier century. Yunnan was a far cry from the seaboard, where the waves of western civilisation had broken into Chinese life and to some extent brought it up-to-date in a western sense. But in that inland walled city all was primitive and eastern. The only means of transport was still coolie or packhorse, and the staple articles of food for its citizens were grown on the surrounding plain.

Except for a few missionaries attached to the C.I.M., the whole of the province was untouched by the Gospel, while western travellers, merchants or government officials were scarcely ever seen at such a great distance from the coast. It will be seen that the United

Sam Pollard of Yunnan

Methodist Mission, in selecting the province of Yunnan and Szechwan for their China mission field, had chosen virgin soil. Pollard was therefore a pathfinder whose work had to be experimental to a very considerable degree. Nor were they in a land of primeval savagery where the white missionary, as a representative of European civilisation, would be received with awe and respect. On the contrary, Europeans were regarded by most of the Chinese as barbarians and uncivilised folk, who had forced their way into a land whose ancient civilisation had everything to teach and nothing to learn.

From his earliest contacts with the Chinese, Sam had sensed this superior attitude, and had determined to master, not merely the Chinese language, but its ancient classics and religious literature as well. By the time Yunnan was reached he had progressed sufficiently in these studies to have a profound admiration for Chinese learning, but none whatever for their way of living. Writing home at this time, he says:

"I have been reading one of the books of Confucius. What a lot of light these people received, but what little influence it has had on their hearts! Yesterday I read the sentence, 'What you do not wish for yourselves, do not give to others.'"

Everywhere he found a deep respect for learning and at the same time an all-pervading darkness of superstition, ignorance and evil. Little wonder that he felt that the first and

Pioneering with Gong and Cornet

urgent duty was to make a determined frontal attack on the forces of evil and ignorance, and to capture as many individuals for Christ as possible. With headstrong but sublime courage, within three weeks of his arrival he planned a ten-days' evangelistic mission in the capital, in conjunction with some C.I.M. missionaries. A week of prayer, and the distribution of thousands of handbills, prepared the way for the special services. From the outset crowds came to the meetings, which were held almost continuously throughout the ten days. Many Chinese seemed deeply impressed by the Gospel message, and several openly professed a desire to serve Jesus Christ.

"Tuesday, the ninth day, we spent in fasting, and this was followed by a night of prayer," says Pollard. "I shall never forget it. Our room was filled with glory, and I had a manifestation such as I had never realised before. The glory came down and so filled me that I felt the Holy Ghost from my head to the soles of my feet. It was about as much as I could stand, and for a minute I thought I should faint or die. I had the promise at that meeting that we were going to have thousands of souls."

We can see now that Pollard was absolutely right over that promise—but he did not realise that it would be a matter of years, not days, before those thousands of souls could be garnered for the kingdom. A few days later he rejoiced in the baptism of their first three converts, but after that had to possess

Sam Pollard of Yunnan

his soul in patience. Meanwhile he wrote to the Missionary Committee at home a glowing account of this promising beginning, and, with the enthusiasm and fine audacity that is characteristic of youth, asked for fifteen to twenty missionaries forthwith to occupy the large towns in the province. Let no one think, however, that Sam's "heart ran away with his head," even in those early pioneering days. Appreciating the Chinese respect for learning and authority, he was careful to "set his cap" at mandarins and leading citizens, a policy that served him in good stead in the adventurous days that followed.

For winning the confidence of the common people he tried other methods, that proved just as effective. About this time, after many talks with Frank Dymond, he deliberately adopted a life of self-denial and poverty, coming down to the level of the coolies and others, not merely wearing Chinese clothes, but living on the frugal and unpalatable fare on which the great mass of the people contrived to exist.

After exploring the city and taking stock of the task that faced them inside the walls and in the suburbs outside, Pollard's next move was to map out the whole district into circuits, or numbered districts, after the manner of the Wesleyan Church at home. Pollard hoped that the time would come when he would see a missionary at work in each circuit, but meanwhile—practical as always—he planned an itinerary through every

Pioneering with Gong and Cornet

circuit at regular intervals, spending a few days in each.

The magnitude and urgency of his task led Pollard to adopt startling, if not sensational, methods. Since he was a teacher with a new message, he felt justified in adopting unheard-of methods for getting a hearing. Picture him, therefore, starting out to visit a distant circuit, carrying a huge Chinese gong. Arriving at a small town he would make his way to the market-place, banging his gong vigorously. Such a strange proceeding was enough to set everyone by the ears. A smile would broaden on the little man's face as he watched a crowd eagerly gathering, obviously bursting with curiosity as to what it all meant. When his following was big enough to satisfy him, the clanging of the gong would suddenly cease, and Pollard would at once begin to preach the Gospel. Some of his friends were horrified at this crude method of publicity, and tried to persuade him to leave the gong at home, and borrow Dymond's concertina instead. As Pollard could only play one tune upon it, he got tired of this method of attracting a crowd before the Chinese did!

Sometimes while journeying round a district or travelling to and from Chaotong, the wildness of this mountainous region added a dash of peril to the going that was appreciated less by other missionaries than by the little man with the gong. On one occasion he was travelling with Samuel Thorne over the mountains, and after a thrilling but dangerous climb, they

Sam Pollard of Yunnan

found themselves facing a swirling, deep-cut river, full of rapids. As they had already had a narrow escape from a ducking through crossing the river higher up in a native boat, they were not anxious to make a second passage. Before long, however, they fervently wished it had been possible to get a boat—the reason can best be explained in Pollard's own words.

. . . .

At " Wild Buffalo " hamlet there was another way of crossing the river—a slide or sling. A bamboo hawser was stretched from the two banks about twenty to forty feet above the water, and on this was suspended a wooden seat. You sit on this, slide down half-way, and are pulled up the other half. Queer travelling this, with a vengeance! The rapids extend a hundred yards above the slide and more than a mile below—boiling, seething whirlpools; waters chasing each other as if mad when they meet one of the many rocks in mid-stream, venting their fury as if they would crush the stone in pieces at one rush! As it happened there was no one to go over before us, so we had no time for reflection, only action.

Our man got on first, and sat on the little seat; they let him go and he swung down half-way and there rested awhile, till those on the other bank gathered in the slack rope and pulled him safely over. About one minute's suspense. Who next?

Sam Thorne and I looked at each other and

Pioneering with Gong and Cornet

asked, shall we go or not? The idea of being swung over these rapids by just one rope was not tempting to either of us. Back comes the seat, so we must decide. If we are to give the people the Gospel, we must not be beaten by a boat or a nasty-looking swing. The seat has arrived; the man in charge says, "Please get on!" I, with my heart far down in my stomach, put my legs on the frame. They put an extra rope round me, lest I should get dizzy in the middle and lose my hold. I clasp my hands over the big wooden ring from which the seat hangs, shut my eyes and swing off.

Down—down—down! Then a stop, and I was dangling over a mile of rocks, whirlpools and rapids. I was too cowardly to look down, and waited until a tug told me the uphill work had begun. A few seconds and I was safely on the other rock, half laughing at myself for being afraid. Back goes the rope and seat, and Sam Thorne, with his burly frame, sits on it. All ready! Yes. Off! Down he slides, and then the uphill work. Pull, pull! Hullo, what's amiss? Snap goes the pulling-rope, and there is Sam dangling in the centre!

I was more frightened than he was. Those on the other side began to pull him back. What if that rope break also? I felt very queer about it! They pulled Sam Thorne back safely. How will they manage now? Will Sam give it up and not try again? Then one of the men sat on the seat and pulled himself across, hand over hand. The rope is tied again, and back goes the seat. Will Sam venture or not? Yes.

Sam Pollard of Yunnan

He takes his seat again, and this time is pulled over in safety. I clap and call Sam an example of British pluck.

. . . .

As Pollard's work progressed, he was able to get help in his journeys from one of their first converts, James Yang, who had made such progress in the new faith that he was now appointed native evangelist to the mission. The missionary and Yang travelled side by side, the former on a mule, the latter on Shanks' pony. Following them came a coolie carrying their baggage and stock in trade: " three hundred Gospels and other books, nine hundred tracts, a piece of salt, some tea, lard, native sauce, a gong, a pair of Chinese Wellingtons, a thousand cash, twelve shillings in silver (specie), an extra pair of stockings, a quilt, a rug, and a few Chinese cakes."

When they arrived at a market called " The Dragon's Head," Yang secured the corner of an opium stall for spreading out his books for sale, while Pollard went on to a piece of high ground facing the crowded market square. No one took the slightest notice of either of them until suddenly—" Clang, clang, clang ! "

The raucous sound of the gong startled everybody. The busy crowd halted in its activity, and turned round to see what was happening. People who had seen the little man with his gong before turned stolidly away, but others came running up to hear his story.

Then down came the rain, scattering the

Pioneering with Gong and Cornet

crowd pell-mell. Pollard took refuge in a tea-shop where a gambling table was a source of great attraction. The missionary watched the two men in charge as they swindled the coppers from some boys, until he could stand it no longer. Pushing to the front, he told the men what he thought of them and their swindling tricks in no measured terms.

By this time the rain had stopped, so they went on to the next market, this time called "The Dragon's Pool," where the gong clamorously called the busy people to listen to the preacher's story. Here an audience of nearly eight hundred squatted down and listened patiently to all Pollard had to say. Next day their road wound through a dark and silent fir forest that proved very uncanny travelling, and six pedlars that they overtook one after another were glad to join their party.

As the shadows of evening fell they reached a patch of road " as steep as the roof of a house," with a big drop on either side that would have ended the journeying of any member of the party who had stumbled. Picking their way by the light of Pollard's lantern the three of them crept cautiously on, followed by the pedlars. They reached an inn at last, and soon forgot their troubles around its blazing fire. The innkeeper's wife talked " a hundred to the dozen," according to Pollard, jabbering so fast that he commented, " Poor husband ! "

During that journey they travelled over eighty miles, visited five markets, preached in

Sam Pollard of Yunnan

six villages, sold two hundred books, and gave away hundreds of tracts—all for a sum of six shillings for expenses for the whole party.

So the work went on from month to month, not without taking its toll of the health and strength of the tireless missionary. The following incident in a barber's shop reminds us that even at this time Pollard's work was performed under the threat of periodic heart attacks that warned him to husband his physical resources.

"On my way back from Tungch'uan," he says, "I called to have a shave. Whilst being tortured by the barber my old feeling came on, and I presently awoke to find myself lying on the mud-floor trying to remember what I had been dreaming about. I was sweating all over. The situation struck me: I had fainted in the heart of China—and I had the cheek to say in Chinese: 'This is my thorn in the flesh.'"

About this time something happened that was to affect the whole of Pollard's after-life and work. Perhaps, under the providence of God, it occurred at this time to provide the necessary care for his health. On the other side of the city stood the mission-house of the China Inland Mission, and thither, early in 1890, had come a young English missionary named Emma Hainge. As a result of friendly conference and social intercourse with the other missionaries, Sam fell deeply in love with her. As usual he was impatient and impetuous, and soon became very anxious to test the lady's feelings towards him, so he sent a note across

Pioneering with Gong and Cornet

to the other Mission House and waited feverishly for a reply. There is a very human little note in his journal that day (March 5th, 1890):

"I calculated about the time she would be home, and got down on my knees and prayed. Didn't I feel bad! What a morning I spent! After service I found a note addressed to me on my table. All right! Hallelujah! We had a long talk together in the evening at her house. When I returned I took her photo with me, and sat down and wrote another letter. Oh, Sam Pollard! Tell it not in Gath! Gone! Irretrievably gone!! But I am glad to be gone!"

That Emma Hainge succumbed to Sam's devoted attentions was not surprising, for at that time he presented a most attractive figure for any woman, with his massive forehead, large, thoughtful eyes, and a bloom as of a ripening peach on his cheeks. He wore a long, pale blue, well-laundered cotton gown, and as protection from the heat, a finely-plaited, large-brimmed straw hat, lined with pale blue, and fastened under the chin, as the crown was small, with blue ribbon strings. He looked quite pretty, and the C.I.M. ladies amongst themselves sometimes called him "the dairymaid."

Sam was an ardent lover, but had to wait patiently until September before he could become formally engaged, for the lady of his choice insisted on securing the consent of her parents. By the end of the year they were married, travelling to Chungking for the purpose.

Sam Pollard of Yunnan

By this time, however, death had visited the ranks of the little band of missionaries, and a re-distribution of their forces became necessary. Samuel Thorne had passed to higher service, Thomas Vanstone was broken in health, while of two new recruits—John Carter and William Tremberth—sent out in response to Pollard's urgent request—the former had died almost on arrival. It was therefore decided that Pollard and his wife should take charge of the work at Chaotong.

Although regretting the change Pollard found the work at Chaotong very much to his liking. For one thing the city was busier than the more remote centre of Yunnan Fu, and the mission work was more developed. The mission house was known to the Chinese by the significant name of "The Hall of Happiness." But if there was more life at Chaotong, the missionary found that anti-foreign feeling was much more intense. He was sneered at openly in the streets as a "foreign devil" and—what was not so easily endured—men spat on the ground and women covered their noses when he passed, as though meeting an offensive smell. Yet he worked on undismayed at healing and preaching.

Original as ever, he used the loud blast of a cornet in arresting the attention of the crowds who passed the hired shop where Gospel services were held. If his courteous invitation to enter failed to win a response from those who stopped to listen, the loud strains of the instrument when played inside the building

Pioneering with Gong and Cornet

soon brought in a crowded audience. At one meeting they had an attendance of one hundred and forty-seven people, and many more were not able to get in.

Side by side with the work of preaching went healing of the sick—work that did even more to advertise the mission than the silver-tongued cornet. Day after day a queue of sufferers lined up at the door, expecting cures from rotting leprosy or venereal disease by some magic incantation or secret charm. Many of them were past human help; others were subjects for dangerous and delicate surgical operations far beyond Pollard's skill. Those who could not be cured were sent away soothed and comforted, with a new experience of human pity and a wonderful story of divine love.

Chapter Five

RELIEVING FAMINE AND FACING RIOT

WE can well believe that the vision of the man from Macedonia that came to St. Paul in the night at Troas, had its origin in day-dreams as the apostle looked across the Hellespont to the shores of Europe in the west.

We are reminded of this by a picture in Pollard's journal of the little missionary during a journey from Chaotong to Yongshan, gazing longingly across the river to the mountains of Szechwan, at the homes of the aboriginal Nosu people of south-west China. Coming events must have cast their shadows athwart the turbid waters as Pollard looked eagerly across to the other bank, for he writes in his journal:

"No missionary has ever yet visited these people; the mists never lift from their minds. The river Yangtze is the boundary between their territory and the Chinese. They are fierce mountain clans living under their own chieftains almost independent of the Chinese. . . . They come down from their fastnesses in robber bands and 'lift' the cattle and crops of the Chinese, and steal people for slaves. . . . I would like to go over and spend a month among them."

Occasionally he met some of these Nosu chiefs, always with a feeling, shared by Thomas

Relieving Famine and Facing Riot

Vanstone, that God intended him to work among them sooner or later. But for the time Chaotong and its people demanded all his attention. In July that year (1892) terrific rains and floods spread devastation in many directions. That old tiger, the Yangtze, broke bounds and spread himself far and wide, carrying death and suffering everywhere. Standing on the wall by the south gate of the city, Pollard saw houses falling in all directions, for mud walls crumble rapidly after incessant rain.

We have already seen that the teeming population of the vast plateau was more or less self-supporting, living on local produce. This meant, of course, that the gaunt shadow of famine follows swiftly after a period of incessant rain or extensive flooding. Only three weeks after Pollard had watched the devastating floods from the city wall, a man called at the mission house to offer them his little girl for sale!

His pitiful story was soon told—the floods had destroyed all his crops; he had two other children and an aged mother to keep, and could not earn more than a few cash per day, so his only hope for immediate relief was to sell his eldest daughter. The price he asked was 200 cash. The warm-hearted missionary gave him the cash and told him to keep his daughter. The man's gratitude was touching, but as he departed Pollard and his wife felt a sickening certainty that they had only delayed for a brief time the child's passing into slavery.

Those months of famine lived in Pollard's

Sam Pollard of Yunnan

memory for years. The fatalistic view of life that is common in China seemed to paralyse all efforts to ameliorate the suffering from such a calamity. The burden of finding ways and means of keeping people alive over a wide area fell on the shoulders of Pollard and his wife rather than the local mandarins. The little missionary travelled far and wide, trying to alleviate suffering from his slender resources, but his efforts seemed as fruitless as trying to fill a funnel. Makeshift hovels had been erected to provide some sort of shelter from the biting cold and driving snow, but this seemed to do little more than prolong the agony of slow starvation. Oftentimes Pollard arrived at a village with a small supply of food and money, but was too late with even that slender help.

" At one village we found a miserable family in a dark hovel destitute of all comfort," he reported. " They were two old people over fifty and two boys—one twelve and the other five. They had been without food for several days when someone gave them a small measure of maize. This they cooked and shared among themselves; but the reaction was too much for the man and he died next morning. We found the mother in a dreadful condition. She was lying on the floor with two coats to cover her, and the small boy had nestled close to her for warmth. She could not eat, but asked for medicine. I left some food and money. The next day I sent medicine and more food, but the poor woman had died at midnight."

Relieving Famine and Facing Riot

From the first Emma Pollard had proved a real helpmate to her husband, cheerfully sharing the sacrifices that his voluntary poverty entailed for them both. The mission in Chaotong had now been established for six years, and so far not a single convert had been baptised. Day after day they had to cast their bread upon the waters, with a faith that never faltered. But at times Sam's unfailing fund of humour and high spirits were sorely needed to carry them through.

At last the tide turned. Early in 1893 he was able to purchase a piece of land on which to erect a mission station of their own. When building work had started Sam wrote, " It will make a fine place. I hope to have a chapel where hundreds shall be saved. The Lord help me and all of us to do the very best."

His faith was rewarded sooner than he expected, for *before* the new chapel was completed two converts came forward for baptism. It was a great day of triumph for Sam. The ceremony was performed in the courtyard of the new premises, before a crowd that filled every corner of the place. Sam sent a full report to his father, with pardonable enthusiasm:

" The people behaved splendidly during the sermon. Then came the baptism. We had a straw mat in front of the table at the top of the steps leading to the platform. I called the two catechumens, Yang-K'ai-Yong and Chang Yong Gin, who came up bravely. For once the foreigner ceased to be ' the cynosure of neighbouring eyes '. I began to feel somewhat

Sam Pollard of Yunnan

nervous, and my voice was trembling and husky. We three bared our heads, and I questioned them publicly. The last question was : ' Are you quite willing all your lives to serve God with all your heart and mind ? ' I expected them to answer ' Quite willing.' Yang-K'ai-Yong, however, boldly declared : ' I am perfectly willing my whole life to serve my Lord Jesus fully .' There was a ring of truth and decision about his words which gladdened us all.

"Then we three knelt down before the whole audience, and I prayed to God to accept and keep us His for ever. The two remained kneeling while I rose and baptised them. All eyes watched : all ears listened. God above rejoiced and blessed. Thus were admitted into the (Protestant) Church of Christ the first two Christian converts. God grant a mighty army may succeed them ! "

Yang-K'ai-Yong, who had been adopted when a boy by Samuel Thorne, had been prayed for night after night by that missionary, and also by Sam Pollard, for whom Yong now acted as servant. Needless to say, he proved an even better servant after his conversion.

Chang Yon Gin was called " Everlasting Gold " (a translation of his Christian name), and soon became a successful preacher of the Gospel.

"He had that which the old Methodists called *the fire*," writes Mrs. Pollard. " He was very successful as an evangelist amongst the villagers ; I have seen him after a ' good time '

Relieving Famine and Facing Riot

throw his hat in the air and shout ' Hallelujah ! ' His mother was a Buddhist witch and opium smoker, and by God's help he lifted her above this sordid plane and led her in the path of those who wished to follow Jesus Christ. After her death he went to Yunnan Fu to help Mr. Allen of the C.I.M. in his work amongst the numerous villages surrounding the city."

This *annus mirabilis* ended in a great triumph for Pollard. The new chapel was formally opened for worship on Christmas Sunday, and on the following day the event was celebrated by a Christmas feast in proper Chinese fashion.

With the new year the Pollards were reluctantly forced to leave Chaotong for a furlough at Tungch-uan, a little city among the hills on the road between Chaotong and Yunnan Fu. An attack of malaria and superintending the new building had drained the strength of the little missionary. Here their first son was born. A furlough in England followed, but towards the end of 1896 the Pollards left English shores for south-west China, reaching Chaotong in the following April.

With health restored and a confidence born of experience, Sam threw himself into his second term of missionary work with fierce energy and great acumen. Without neglecting the illiterate masses he took pains to cultivate the friendship of the mandarins and leading people of the city. He tried to persuade the learned people of the district to accept the Gospel, and distributed books among the students who

Sam Pollard of Yunnan

came up for the triennial examinations. He conducted an elementary school, distributed Western books and Chinese newspapers, and lectured on Western science. In addition to all this he preached the Gospel and his simple medical work went on unceasingly. Thus by all ways of approach to all sorts of people he was making friends for himself and the mission, and unconsciously safeguarding the future.

One day a Chinese student belonging to a family in good circumstances came to the Chaotong mission in great distress. To Pollard's amazement the young man's trouble was not physical or mental, but entirely spiritual. He had just arrived from Yunnan Fu, where the mission station was in charge of Dr. Lewis Savin, whose medical skill had done great things for the mission, and by whom the student had been put under a deep conviction of sin. At their first meeting Pollard and the student—whose name was Stephen Li (Lee)—were attracted to each other like David and Jonathan. The friendship thus begun between the two men overswept all barriers of race and upbringing. The new friends sat and talked far into the night, and before they parted had found another source of fellowship, for Pollard won Lee for his Master, Jesus Christ. A few days later Stephen brought his elder brother, John, to Pollard, and in time the whole family became Christians, and the two brothers served the mission as teachers and preachers. It is interesting to read Stephen Li's impression of his English friend:

Relieving Famine and Facing Riot

"Seeing Mr. Pollard's deeds and hearing his speech, I judged that we had in China one who was unique. As I learned to know him, I greatly admired the spirit that was in him: it was almost like seeing one of our sages reincarnated. After leading my elder brother into the church, we discussed with Mr. Pollard the whole question of education, and the result was that the Mission school was transformed. It became the fountain-head of the Western learning in the province of Yunnan. Mr. Pollard taught arithmetic, geography, music and drill, whilst all other schools remained in the old ruts and our scholars continued to dream. The Western teacher looked upon my brother and me as his hands and feet. We loved each other with virtue and courtesy."

Then came the first mutterings of the Boxer storm, that was to echo throughout the world and bring martyrdom to thousands of Christians in China, foreign and native. The origin of the anti-foreign movement called Boxerism cannot be described in detail here. Suffice it to say that the growing impact of Western civilisation on unwilling China resulted in a widening cleavage between the more progressive people who welcomed reforms of all kinds, and the conservative and reactionary majority who stood by the old policy of "China for the Chinese, and keep out all barbarian foreigners." Supporters of the old order looked upon Christianity as the prime mover of every reform.

At first the trouble began with local upheavals and sporadic risings in various parts of

Sam Pollard of Yunnan

the great empire. Then the storm burst in western China, where a Mantsi coalminer organised a revolt. He announced his intention of marching throughout China, destroying all Christians as he went. As Chaotong was near the scene of this rising, the city became seething with excitement at once. It was reported that the rebel leader would enter the city within five days. Immediately the services at the new chapel were deserted by most of the people, and Pollard was urged to flee. Instead, however, the little missionary and his brave wife and family—by this time a second son had arrived—lived on as though nothing were about to happen. The spirit of our hero is revealed by the fact that he chose this moment to send out two of his best native preachers on an evangelistic tour among the villages, and started a weekly prayer-meeting at the mission house.

During the following days sensation followed sensation. Hundreds of men in the districts round the city were said to be in league with the rebels, and had sworn a solemn oath not to rest until all the Christians were exterminated. One morning Pollard found a notice fixed to his front door, announcing that the 29th day of the month had been fixed for killing the missionaries. With a smile of scorn he tore the notice down and went on with his work.

"The twenty-ninth came: the big doors were kept open as usual and as late as on other days," reported Pollard. "A great quiet came over the city for a short time, which was broken later by the incessant firing of crackers and the

Relieving Famine and Facing Riot

barking of dogs. Unknown to us, soldiers were keeping special guard in the neighbourhood, and the officer in charge, a friend of ours, had no sleep that night. I did not get much either. The morning broke with warm, clear sunshine, and at eight o'clock the prefect called to wish us the Chinese equivalent of a happy New Year. In the midst of all this unrest we were well, happy and scarcely disturbed in our spirits at all. We felt sure that God was with us. Our New Year's mail brought news of the murder of two more missionaries, and advice from a friend down the river to make preparations for flight. I hear my bonny boy laughing heartily outside, and my wife singing at the organ. Good-bye!"

A few months later the Chinese were amazed to see a British Army officer, his Indian attendants, and a black cook riding through the streets of Chaotong. Strange visitors were rare in that part of China, so that such a variety of nationalities caused quite a sensation. Pollard invited the officer and his party to be his guests for the night. He found that Lieutenant Watts-Jones was conducting a railway survey for the Burma-Yunnan Railway Survey Commission, and had spent a fortnight in the province, searching for a suitable route for the proposed iron road. It was natural that his talk with Pollard should last far into the night. Next morning the party left early, and for Pollard the visit became nothing more than a pleasant memory. But it had an unpleasant sequel that nearly ended in his assassination!

Sam Pollard of Yunnan

The number of visitors to the mission-house at once increased by leaps and bounds, and Sam was naturally much encouraged at this interest shown in their work. Then came disillusionment. He discovered that the populace believed that the black cook was still at the mission house, and a rumour had been spread that he was being fed by the missionary on Chinese babies! This was solemnly believed by all classes, with the result that women and children were in terror, and men vowed that they would not only kill the cannibal ogre, but the foreigners as well. An angry demonstration took place outside Pollard's house, the leaders of the mob crying, "The foreigners eat the children." Some of the crowd wanted to beat their way into the house and kill the inhabitants on the spot, but for some reason they were restrained.

A few nights later, however, a plot was hatched by some of their enemies. It was a pitch-black night, and after the usual evening service Pollard and Yang, the native evangelist, stood by the big gate that led into the street, watching the last of the worshippers groping their way down the unlighted road, guided by the fitful light of lanterns. The mission courtyard was enveloped in darkness, and feeling their way, Sam and the evangelist closed the big gate for the night and swung the cross-bar into position. Sam was the first to grope his way back into the courtyard, little thinking as he passed the corner of the porch that an assassin, armed with a sharp dagger, was

Relieving Famine and Facing Riot

waiting in the darkness to stab him. Whether the Englishman's soft footfall escaped the ear of the would-be murderer, or whether the man mistook his quarry will never be known, but Sam passed the dark corner safely and felt his way towards the house.

Suddenly a wild scream rang out behind him, followed by a shout and a scurrying of feet. At once the whole household was alarmed, for nerves had been on edge for several days owing to the threats of the crowd. Hurrying across the courtyard with a light, Emma Pollard was relieved to see her husband safe and sound; but across the porch lay the form of the evangelist in a pool of blood. The lurking assassin had stabbed his own countryman, and the hated foreigner had escaped unharmed. Upon examination they found that Yang was wounded in four places, on his arm and chest. Without doubt he owed his life to the thick wadded coat he wore. As Pollard was wearing a thin cotton gown at the time, it is clear that but for the mistake of the assassin our story would have come to an end here.

For the next twelve months Pollard took advantage of a temporary lull in the rising Boxer storm by " digging himself in " more effectively at Chaotong. He advised the prefect to urge the people to grow wheat, beans and maize to forestall an approaching food shortage, and that official was glad enough to accept and act upon the suggestion. Greatly daring, the missionary also made two preaching tours in the district, visiting the principal markets on

Sam Pollard of Yunnan

the way, singing, playing on his concertina, and preaching for hours, trying to make friends with all classes of people.

The Boxer storm burst in the middle of 1900, and missionaries in China had to flee for their lives. Fortunately the viceroys of the southern provinces were more enlightened than the Empress Dowager and her Grand Council. In promulgating the imperial edict "Kill all foreigners," these viceroys altered the verb "kill" to "protect," so that its original purpose was not carried out in the south. All the missionaries, however, were ordered by their consuls to leave the interior. Finding that this order had to be obeyed, Pollard placed the work at Chaotong in charge of the evangelist Yang, and the teacher Stephen Li, and retired from the city. In this crisis his firm friendship with the prefect and mandarins served the whole party in good stead, for they had a military escort to protect them. They reached Hong Kong in safety, and spent the next few months in Shanghai.

Unable to be idle, Pollard took a leading part in cleansing one of the principal thoroughfares of immoral traffic at night. He also gained some notoriety, and not a little unpopularity, by his outspoken denunciation of the British traffic in opium.

Chapter Six   **BACK IN YUNNAN**

IT is not our purpose to trace the course of the Boxer riots and the European armed intervention that followed. Although Pollard did his best to serve his Master at Shanghai, his heart was all the while in Yunnan, and as the months passed he chafed at the fetters that bound him to the coast.

At last on February 9th, 1901, he started joyfully with his wife, two children and a lady missionary on the first stage of their return to the interior. They had official sanction to go as far as Chungking, but the date of their return to Yunnan itself was still problematic. After a fortnight's fruitless effort to get permission for the whole party to go on to Chaotong, Pollard was forced to leave the ladies and children at Chungking, and travel on alone.

The last stages of his journey proved a triumphal progress. Five miles from the city he was met by a cheering crowd bearing a huge card of "greeting and welcome from church members, members on trial, and inquirers." Strings of crackers were let off to bang their welcome, and a wayside feast was spread in a neighbouring farmhouse. Eventually Pollard entered Chaotong like a king returning to his capital. The procession was headed by twenty scroll-banners and a huge presentation tablet, while the streets were lined with staring people.

Sam Pollard of Yunnan

The latter looked so serious that only with difficulty could the irrepressible Pollard remain seated solemnly in his sedan chair and preserve the gravity suited to such an occasion in China.

The chief satisfaction to Pollard, in such a public welcome, was the publicity it gave to the mission. Although the Christian Church at Chaotong had survived the Boxer crisis through the untiring devotion of its native leaders, Sam was greatly disappointed with the condition of affairs awaiting him. He candidly admits that, had it not been possible to return, the Church would have been defunct in a few years.

Be that as it may, the Boxer rebellion marked a great change in the condition of China, especially as regards the work of missionaries like Pollard. In all directions the people were anxious to receive missionaries, and get a knowledge of the Christian religion. The old hostility or indifference to the " Jesus-religion " had passed away for a time. For Pollard, too, the rebellion had brought changes. Close contact with other missionaries and the European community at Shanghai had broadened his outlook and deepened his sense of responsibility. He took up his duties at Chaotong with new ideas, bolder plans, and greater confidence.

He still gazed wistfully across the river to the distant mountains of Szechwan, and looked forward to the time when he could do pioneer work among the aborigines. But meantime he planned a series of important preaching journeys

Back in Yunnan

over a wide area in north-east Yunnan. Their purpose was for exploring the missionary possibilities after the collapse of Boxerism.

On these five great tours Pollard was careful to take with him native workers for training; Mr. Yen, an evangelist; John Li, the schoolmaster; and Chong-Ming-Tsai, a candidate for the ministry. At each place visited they found that the leading citizens were inquirers, while the masses of the people were so eager to be taught the Christian faith that Pollard suspected at first there were unworthy motives prompting them. As a result of this first tour he reported :

" Hundreds of people gave in their names as inquirers, representing a community of many thousands; three chapels were formally opened; three others are in course of preparation. Writing now six weeks after our return, and after hearing the report of Mr. Yen and Mr. Wang, who are also back, the whole movement seems marvellous. In this prefecture of Chaotong there are people from thirty-four places asking us to teach them. Most of them are Chinese; but some are Mahommedans, some are Miao, and some are I-ren. Nearly all are absolutely ignorant of what real Christianity is; some are moved by impure, selfish motives; but in the movement there is the hand of God plainly seen."

A second tour followed six weeks after the first, and took Pollard into wilder regions that not only taxed his endurance but tested his courage. His journal gives many a " pocket-

Sam Pollard of Yunnan

camera picture " of scenes and incidents on this missionary exploration. Of these the following is typical :

"Yesterday we crossed the Fairy Bridge, five li the other side of Chong-ts'uen at Kiohpan-ai; it is built on the side of a cliff, and consists of huge slabs of stone resting on supports which have been driven right into the cliff. It was only when one looked through the cracks that one became aware of the black chasm below. The people said no mortals could have made such a road; it could only have been made by fairies. Once the road wound round the middle of a cliff with a big fall: a railing of stone bounded part of the pathway, but in many parts this had broken away, and I held my breath as I passed along. After fifty li we came down to Huei Ch'i on the Yangtze. At this place the river narrows and forms a dangerous rapid. As we were watching, a small boat-load of coolies came down. It was exciting to see them shoot the rapid; but they got over safely."

Wherever they went the hunger of people for the Gospel was remarkable. Looking back at this period, we can see now that had the Christian Church in England risen to its opportunities, the Chinese Empire might at that time have been captured for Christianity. In several places Pollard's inability to settle down there and then as a resident missionary caused deep disappointment and chagrin. In one village two hundred people gathered to hear the Gospel story, and were so attracted by it

Back in Yunnan

that they offered to pay him to remain as their professional teacher. Indeed, an enthusiastic member of the crowd collected a large sum of money on the spot, and offered it to Pollard as a guarantee of good faith.

A third grand tour followed early in 1902, and again Pollard and his native assistants found it impossible to cope with the crowds of inquirers. Steadily pursuing a settled policy, Sam used his native assistants more and more, with the object of training them to take charge of village stations. In some places chapels were provided by the inquirers themselves. One day Pollard was invited to open a chapel that some " believing disciples " (their own term) had secured at Fu-Kuan-Ts'uen. As he approached the city he was met by several Chinese graduates in full dress. Soon afterwards came a messenger bearing the mandarin's card of welcome. For the final stage he was accorded a military escort of twenty soldiers.

By the time the city gate was reached Pollard found himself accompanied by quite a formidable procession. As he entered the city thousands of crackers were let off, and thousands of people watched the little missionary march in. Tea was served at a large inn, and after it was over Pollard and his friends preached from three tables to different sections of the large crowd. Soldiers kept guard and played the first and second watch signals and then sounded " Lights out." For the missionary it was a noisy, tiring, trying, but happy day.

Between these grand tours Sam worked hard

Sam Pollard of Yunnan

to strengthen and extend the work at Chaotong. A school for the training of native teachers, founded at Tungch-uan in 1900, had been transferred to Chaotong, and was developing apace. The medical work of Dr. Savin was increasing so rapidly that a site had to be acquired for building a hospital. Mr. Yen and Stephen Li had been settled at two outstations, Lao-wa-t'an and Fu-Kuan-Ts'uen, and were doing excellent work under Pollard's supervision.

One unlooked-for result of these exploratory tours throughout north-east Yunnan was the frequent contact Pollard secured with the Nosu from across the Yangtze. This rekindled his earlier hopes and ambitions to cross the Yellow River and penetrate the forbidden land of the Nosu. This would be a hazardous undertaking, through opposition by the Chinese on that side of the river, apart from the dangers that lay concealed in the forbidden land itself. Here is Pollard's description of the situation:

" Nosu chiefs have for generations defied all the efforts of the Chinese to conquer their country. They have made the mountains their home, and here they live a free bold life, ready to fight all comers, and willing to sacrifice their lives in defence of their highland homes. They laugh at the Chinese as an effeminate race, who dwell in towns and love peace. With them the brave man is the hero, and the only man who can make sure of keeping what he possesses, by being ever ready to fight anybody about anything.

Back in Yunnan

"The River Yangtze flows between Nosuland and the prefecture of Chaotong. The Yangtze in those parts is a fierce unnavigable river, as bold and dashing as the highlander among the eternal hills, and as ready to avenge to the death the insults of any who dare to treat it lightly by attempting to travel down its deep-flowing waters. Now and again, conscious of its great strength, it settles down quietly and half goes to sleep, and in these places men are quick to cross from bank to bank in ferry boats.

"On one side of the Yangtze, where the Chinese live, there are rich farms, wealthy farmsteads, and large market villages giving evidence of prosperity and wealth. The hillsides are dotted with white towers, which remind one of old baronial castles, and the warfare of feudal days. These white towers are built for defence against the tribesmen, who dwell in Nosuland. There have been perpetual feuds between the various tribes of Nosuland, and again between the hillmen on one side of the Yangtze and the Chinese on the other.

"The tribes are always ready for a border raid. In each house weapons are kept hanging on the wall, and by their side are suspended bags of oatmeal, containing, in addition to the meal, a thin copper basin and a wooden spoon. When the horn sounds from the Big House or Castle, all the men in the homes nearby seize their weapons and their bags of meal, and in an incredibly short time large forces are mustered

Sam Pollard of Yunnan

at central places, fully equipped for a raid of four or five days' duration."

The Nosu in their mountain homes live under a feudal system that probably dates back many centuries, and was adopted for self-preservation. The princes or feudal lords who own the soil are called Earth Eyes. They are served by the Black Bloods, serfs who work the land for the Earth Eyes in return for protection. Below these are the White Bloods, or slaves. A large proportion of the White Bloods are not Nosu at all, but Miao—another aboriginal people scattered throughout Yunnan and Kweichow. They are an inferior and less warlike race than the Nosu, and have not succeeded in retaining their independence, so have passed under the domination of both the Nosu and the Chinese.

Although the Chinese authorities would not allow people to cross the river into Nosuland, they could not blind themselves to the advantages of allowing Nosu traders to come into Yunnan for purposes of barter. Hence it came about that from time to time Pollard had encountered Nosu people around Chaotong. The fact that the authorities forbade travellers to enter Nosuland increased his desire to journey into the forbidden territory, although he knew that to venture across without a guide would be to ask for death or slavery. Imagine, therefore, his delight when he became friendly with Long, a Nosu chief living in his district, who was in constant touch with other chiefs living across the river.

Chapter Seven **ENTERING THE FORBIDDEN LAND.**

"WHERE is he off to now?" said a Chinese merchant to a friend, as they watched Sam Pollard slip furtively out of the gate of Chaotong early one morning.

"Who knows the plans of these foreigners?" replied the other Chinese darkly. "He is taking that Nosu chief somewhere."

Well might the Chinese people speculate as to Pollard's destination on that November morning. After a lingering farewell to his wife and family, he had hurried off with Chief Long on the most desperate venture he had yet attempted in China. Ostensibly he was going to visit the home of this Nosu chief at T'oh-chee, three days' journey distant. This was the official plan, but there was a secret known only to three persons that made the parting a tense one. After much trouble, Pollard had persuaded Chief Long to take him across the river to the Great Cold Mountains. In other words the intrepid missionary was starting out for forbidden Nosuland.

Pollard made light of the danger, for to him this was the beginning of the realisation of a long-cherished dream. For those Great Cold Mountains—forbidding, unexplored, mysterious —had beckoned to him year after year, and he had promised himself that one day he would explore their secrets.

Sam Pollard of Yunnan

Once Chaotong was left behind he talked freely to his guide about the prospects of their journey. Both men laughed as Pollard retailed the weird and wonderful stories that the Chinese told about the wild men of the Nosu hills, whom they dubbed Lolo or Man-tsz—native names with an uncomplimentary meaning much resented by the Nosu. Long's father had been an important chief in Nosuland, but he had been killed in the great Mahommedan rebellion, and the family estates seized. With obvious pride, Long described how his mother had rallied the family retainers, after sending her infant sons into hiding, and had ceaselessly fought to regain the family estates almost inch by inch. This Nosu Boadicea had not hesitated in one desperate encounter to lead her forces in person, and take deadly toll of the enemy with her gun. She had lived to see her elder son re-established in the family estates, and her other son, Chief Long, settled in prosperous circumstances at T'oh-chee, on the Chinese side of the Yangtze.

Pollard spent several days in Chief Long's house, which was in reality a walled estate, then started with Long, and a dozen armed men for Nosuland. The hazards of the enterprise were clearly understood by everybody. The fact that the missionary insisted on taking his telescope and camera instead of weapons, instead of proving that his errand was peaceful, simply made him a more terrible foe in the eyes of Long's people. Sam was amused to find that his telescope was looked upon as " a

Entering the Forbidden Land

terrible thousand-mile gun, able to shoot all that could be seen through it, and never going off unless there were sufficient people opposed to us to make it worth while firing. As to my camera, when that was fixed on the tripod, and the missionary disappeared under the cloth, no Gatling gun nor any of its numerous offspring could have caused greater consternation. We were going among a people who, with all their bravery and contempt for the Chinese, are absolutely in the hands of the wizards, and terribly afraid of magic and demons. I was presumed to be an expert in all matters concerning the black art, and even those who wished to rob our party were much too scared to run the risk."

Towards the end of the first day, they reached the banks of the Yangtze. As the river forms the border between Yunnan and Nosuland, it was zealously guarded by the Chinese. Pollard had hoped to get across the river without difficulty, by keeping his real plans secret when leaving Chaotong. At the river's brink, however, it became clear that his secret had leaked out, for the Chinese authorities had ordered the ferrymen to prevent the foreigner crossing at all costs. In characteristic fashion the captain in charge of the ferry first tried the gentle art of persuasion. When this failed he offered Pollard presents of rice, pork, and oranges. As this bribe did not succeed, secret instructions were issued to knock the bottom out of the only ferry boat available, so as to make the crossing impossible. Fortunately, however, the boatmen refused to destroy their

Sam Pollard of Yunnan

property. Unable to stop Pollard by any means, the Chinese official sent word to the tribesmen that the approaching travellers were dangerous, and should either be killed out of hand or held for a big ransom.

Thus literally taking his life into his hands, Pollard crossed the Yangtze next morning because he could not be prevented, and so entered at last the forbidden land of the Nosu. His first experience was not impressive. After leaving the river bank, Chief Long led the party up a narrow gorge that at first glance looked quite impassable. Sometimes the path was nothing more than a few ledges cut in the sloping rock. At other times a log was thrown against the cliff and a few notches cut in it to help the climbers. At several places logs were placed from ledge to ledge, to form a bridge, and over these they had to walk or crawl. A stream was crossed by the rudest of rustic bridges, and Pollard was amused to see Chief Long, who would ride a horse almost anywhere, afraid to trust his legs on these bridges. He crawled over on his hands and knees, shaking all the time.

Only twelve miles were covered on that first day, and they spent the night in a tiny hamlet belonging to a nephew of Chief Long. Next morning they prepared to start early, but Vri-ha, a local chief, who had heard of their arrival, called to see them and insisted on sending for a fat goat to provide a meal in their honour. This meant no further progress till midday. Pollard spent the time talking to Vri-ha, and showing the assembled company

Entering the Forbidden Land

the wonders of a folding chair, a small iron puzzle, and a couple of working figures that caused roars of laughter. He learned casually that Vri-ha had been mixed up in the Chinese plot to kill or capture him, but later, on discovering who Pollard's escort was, the chief had turned right round. Vri-ha now declared that had he been informed of Pollard's arrival on that side of the river, he would have provided a force of six hundred armed men as a bodyguard. Pollard thanked God that he had brought a Nosu chief as his guide.

At noon a fresh start was made, with better progress than on the first day, although in one place the path led over a dizzy height where Pollard declared that "even monkeys put on sandals before they venture to walk over its slippery sides!" The night was spent in a large village that rejoiced in the name of Chie-Tsu-Leh-Chieh, and was surrounded by a strong wall. The smaller houses were low hovels roofed with grass, the better dwelling being tiled with strips of bark. The party were welcomed at one of the larger houses, and as it was very cold, Pollard appreciated being given the place of honour on a wicker-work mat in front of a blazing fire in the long main room of the house. While warming himself in anticipation of the evening meal, a commotion at the farther end of the room aroused his curiosity. Several servants were dragging in a large goat, and to Pollard's disgust the men proceeded to kill and dress the animal for his supper. Chief Long explained afterwards that this repulsive custom was a point of honour with the Nosu, and constituted a guarantee that a fresh animal was killed specially for each party of guests.

"The legs of the goat were the property of the children, who burnt them in a wood fire till all the hair was gone, and then ate their share of the feast with evident relish," wrote Pollard in his journal. "As soon as possible the heart, lungs, liver, etc., were thrown into the burning ashes and after being cooked there for a short time, were placed on a plate for Chief Long and myself, as a special delicacy . . . As soon as the word went forth that the meal was ready, all was bustle and excitement. Sleepers were awakened. Hungry men began to revive their hopes, and the visiting missionary was on the *qui vive.* Several of the retainers stood round, holding up blazing torches of pinewood or dried bamboo. A small wooden trencher, standing about twelve inches from the ground, and carved out of a solid tree-trunk, was placed in front of the two chief guests. On it were placed three wooden basins, one for rice, which was piled up like a pyramid, another for meat, and a third for gravy. All were made of camphor wood. Two wooden spoons completed the outfit, and the guests were bidden to eat heartily. Sometimes the pieces of meat we had were over a pound in weight, and only spoons were provided to eat them with ! The retainers of the guests shared in the meal, and all that remained over was eaten by the retainers of the host."

Entering the Forbidden Land

When the repast was ended, Pollard showed his lantern slides, first of English life, then of the Gospel stories, to an audience that were literally spellbound. Chief Long explained the pictures in the Nosu tongue. Exactly the sort of Gospel that he preached was unknown to Pollard, although the ejaculations of pleasure and wonder, and the outbursts of laughter, gave him furiously to think.

The journey was resumed early next morning in a snow storm. Wherever they went the people were amazed to see a foreigner, and Pollard enjoyed the joke when Chief Long informed people, that this remarkable visitor was " a man bear." The missionary confirmed this description by playfully hugging his guide, and acting occasionally like a performing bear at a circus.

That night they reached the largest village Pollard had yet seen, and were the guests of an old chieftain, Mr. A-Pooh. Pollard had been looking forward to meeting this chief, for Long had described him as a fine old fellow, a mine of Nosu history and rare knowledge. Sam pricked up his ears, for such an authority on Nosu matters would be an ideal host. Alas, they found that A-Pooh had just been visited by a Chinese trader—possibly a spy—who had made the old man a liberal present of wine, with the deplorable result that A-Pooh was so continually drunk that he had no chance of getting sober during the days that the missionary stayed at the house.

They stopped next at a well-fortified village, where an old chief was engaged in a bitter

Sam Pollard of Yunnan

quarrel with another tribe. With pathetic earnestness he begged Pollard to help him by his magic power in the coming battle. In vain did the little missionary protest that he did not possess any magic medicine which could stupefy the enemy when thrown towards him. In the end the old man was comforted by a bright idea.

"Whether you have the magic medicine or not," he said hopefully, "I shall let my enemies know that you have presented me with some, and we will see what happens!"

The sequel to this amusing scheme shows Pollard in the light of an unconscious peacemaker, for the old man's bright idea proved entirely successful. His enemies begged for peace, and sent a present of cattle to secure it, which more than atoned for the injury inflicted during the raid that had started the quarrel.

On another day they reached the home of Vri-ha, the chief who had met them on arrival, and had been turned from an enemy into a friend. As in other places, Pollard was escorted to the place of honour on a mat before the blazing wood fire. Vri-ha's father greeted the visitors warmly. Beside him sat a striking-looking girl of about eighteen; her ears and arms were heavy with coral and amber beads and silver chains, and she was smoking a long pipe. Chief Long whispered that she was Vri-ha's sister, and urged Pollard to take special note of her, accompanying the remark with sly winks and nudges that completely mystified the "man bear." As usual there was much talk and excitement over the stranger's

Entering the Forbidden Land

visit, and the girl near the fire—the only member of her sex present—took the closest possible interest in both Pollard and his affairs.

After the meal Pollard noticed that Vri-ha and Chief Long were in very close conversation on a very important subject. Sometimes they looked at Pollard and smiled at each other; sometimes they looked at the girl by the fire; and Pollard's name was frequently mentioned. Pollard begged them to let him into the secret. It took Long some time to explain matters, and by the time he had finished Pollard's heart was thumping against his ribs, and his hair was almost, if not quite, standing on end!

The little missionary learned that the tribesmen had taken to him very much. Four of the tribes had agreed to recognise him as head chief, and to submit to his ruling on all things. Further, they were willing to adopt Christianity and follow him everywhere. This exalted position could be had by Pollard if he would marry the girl on the other side of the fire, and so make himself a member of the ruling family! Chief Long was warmly in favour of the scheme, said Pollard was a lucky dog, and took it for granted that he would fall in with the proposal. Pollard's first reaction to the proposal was to regard it as a huge joke, but he was quickly assured by Long that the Nosu were in dead earnest over this. They were offering him the greatest honour they could confer on anyone, and it would be dangerous to decline it.

"But what does the girl think of it all?" asked Pollard hopefully, seeing a way out of

Sam Pollard of Yunnan

the dilemma in the maiden's refusal. To the missionary's dismay he was assured that she was not merely willing, but quite eager—and from the way she was regarding him it was quite clear that Chief Long spoke truth!

Pollard was in a fix! Declining to give any immediate answer, he showed his lantern slides with the usual telling effect. But his " heart was in his boots," especially when the lady who had chosen him tried to make friends with him, undeterred by the fact that she could not speak Chinese, and he was a stranger to the Nosu tongue. She seemed to think that he was already her property for she examined his clothes with interest, and even pulled out his necktie to see what it was made of.

For the first time since he had entered Nosuland, Pollard fervently wished himself safely back home. Far into the night he thought round the position, and faced up to the probable results of a false move. To accept was, of course, impossible, but to refuse might have disastrous consequences. His life might not be worth much, but that was nothing compared with the effect his action might have in closing the door against the Gospel. Next morning he was still undecided as to his course of action, but Vri-ha and the would-be bride were keener than ever on the scheme. He began explaining to Vri-ha that he would only be too delighted to have the maiden as a daughter; the English law did not allow him to take a second wife while the first was still living. This might not have gone far with such lawless people, but the

Entering the Forbidden Land

missionary had the presence of mind to add that were he to accept such a great honour, he would bring dishonour upon the maiden. In the end Vri-ha seemed to understand, and Pollard succeeded in getting out of the difficulty without hurting the pride of the host, or prejudicing the Gospel. Nevertheless they insisted on " adopting " him into their family.

Pollard now started homewards, but soon discovered that he had only escaped from one difficult situation by putting himself into another. By being adopted into one of the Nosu clans, he had automatically become an enemy of others. Unfortunately the way home led through the territory of two tribes at enmity with Vri-ha and his people, and plans were made for his capture by a large body of armed men. The Chinese officials, who had been foiled in preventing Pollard from crossing into Nosuland, were parties to the scheme, and the captain of the ferryboat had been bribed not to bring his boat across when Pollard and Long signalled from the Nosu side of the ferry. To add a finishing touch to the plot, news had already been sent to Chaotong that the party had been captured and slain.

All went well with the travellers until they approached the rocky heights overlooking the swift-flowing river that separated them from home and safety. Before descending the gorge, Pollard paused to examine the market-town across the river with his telescope, an act that made a deep impression upon his companions. Unknown to them, it created a still deeper

Sam Pollard of Yunnan

impression upon their enemies, who were watching from their hiding-places, awaiting a favourable opportunity to attack. To all the Nosu people that telescope was a deadly thousand-mile gun, and the enemy was petrified with fear, while Pollard's own men took care to keep well behind him as he used it. They reached the bottom of the gorge in safety, and waited for the ferry-boat to fetch them. But they waited in vain. Their shouts received no answer. After an hour of fruitless shouting they became very impatient and even discussed the possibility of swimming across. Chief Long suspected treachery, a suspicion which became general when enemy scouts were seen watching them intently from a distance. Pollard noticed with dismay that the boulders and rank vegetation around them provided ideal cover whereby a large hostile force could approach them unseen.

A new plan was now tried to galvanize the boatmen into activity. Uncomplimentary remarks about them and their ancestors were flung across the waters with a heartiness that was calculated to sting the unseen boatmen into action of some sort. Still there was no sign of life on the opposite shore, while the enemy on the hilltop gathered in numbers, and seemed to be discussing the best method of attack.

Then the restless Pollard, tired of this inactivity and uncertainty discovered a pastime that all unconsciously saved the situation. Near them was a strip of pebble beach, where a small stream flowed into the Yangtze, and for want of something better to do Pollard

Entering the Forbidden Land

wandered off to it, accompanied by some of their armed guard. At first he began idly throwing stones into the river, and at once his Nosu friends followed suit, and proved themselves adepts at stone-throwing. Put upon his mettle, Sam started throwing up and catching pebbles in quick procession, sometimes having two or three in the air at the same moment and catching them all with unerring precision. This was a new trick to the Nosu, and soon the whole party gathered on the pebble beach to watch the performance with profound admiration. Some of the warriors tried to copy him, but failed completely, catching nasty cracks on their fingers instead.

The fun waxed fast and furious as Pollard, reaping the benefit of long practice in his schooldays, increased the size of the pebbles. The exhibition caught the attention of the enemy forces, who watched the stone-throwing with increasing dread. Before long their superstitious fears of the mysterious magic of the foreigner triumphed over their courage, and they melted away!

Efforts were now redoubled to attract the attention of the ferryboat people. The captain of the ferry had by this time discovered that the kidnapping tribesmen had retired, and realising that the plot had failed, he reluctantly ferried the party across. A few days later a tired but triumphant missionary entered the mission courtyard at Chaotong, where a plucky wife, refusing to believe reports of his death, was hopefully awaiting him.

Chapter Eight. THE COMING OF THE SCOUTS.

POLLARD'S return from the forbidden land of the Great Cold Mountains was a nine day's wonder in Chaotong. Even the prefect of the city openly showed his pleasure when the explorer paid him an official visit in his yamen (official compound) to report his safe return. The mandarins of the city were greatly perturbed over the plots that had threatened him, and it was with difficulty that he dissuaded them from taking steps to punish the offenders. Soon afterwards he was contriving how to enter the forbidden land once more when an event occurred to alter the whole course of his work in China.

One never-to-be-forgotten morning—on July 12th, 1904—four Miao stalked wearily into the mission courtyard. Each was carrying a sack of oatmeal on his shoulder, and with evident relief these were flung on the ground and the men sat on them to rest. For a long time they sat there, looking shyly round them. All sorts and conditions of people came through those big gates, so the coming of these Miao caused no comment. Presently they summoned sufficient courage to enter the inner courtyard and ask meekly,

" Please can we see the teacher ? "

Their request was taken to Pollard, who says:

" In a few moments I went out, and from

The Coming of the Scouts

the upper part of the courtyard looked at my visitors. Little did I dream what it meant for them and for me. Little did any of us dream that this was the revival, come at last. God had smitten the rock and the waters were flowing. But we did not know it then."

Going down into the courtyard, Pollard welcomed the strangers with his usual cordiality. Their spokesman was Chang Mo-shee, and in the course of conversation, the missionary pieced together a remarkable story, although it was weeks before he appreciated its full meaning. Chang Mo-shee and his companions were typical Miao, living on the hills of Kweichow, about two day's journey from Chaotong. Pollard knew that in the corner of the province of Kweichow abutting on Yunnan, the Miao outnumbered the Chinese population many times over. For centuries they had submitted to the domination of the Chinese and Nosu, but lived their own life in their villages on the hills.

Chang Mo-shee told Pollard how scraps of the story of Ie-su [*] had passed from lip to lip among his countrymen, and had stirred their hearts in a mysterious manner. Thirsting to hear more, Chang Mo-shee and others had set out on a quest which was as divinely led as that of the wise men of old. They had tracked the source of the stories of Ie-su to a stranger living in the town of Anshuen. Greatly daring, they journeyed far to see him, and to their amazement were received with gentleness,

[*] The Chinese name for Jesus, pronounced Yea-soo.

Sam Pollard of Yunnan

courtesy and love. Their quest had led them to the mission house of J. R. Adam of the China Inland Mission, who had been working with great success among both Chinese and aborigines for some years in Kweichow. Chang Mo-shee and his friends stayed long enough to learn that the truth about Ie-su was even more wonderful than the stories they had heard.

Finding that these Miao lived near Chaotong, Mr. Adam advised them to go to the English teacher there to learn more about Ie-su. So they had come—and to stay.

Now it so happened (if one can use the term in such circumstances) that a two-storey building stood empty at this time just inside the mission gateway. It had been vacated by Chinese schoolboys because a new school had been built for them near the east gate of the city, and no decision had been arrived at as to its use. As the Miao were unwilling to go to a Chinese inn, to be snubbed and despised, Pollard offered them the empty schoolroom to sleep in. This was eagerly accepted. Straw mattresses were provided, and they lived comfortably for several days, drinking in eagerly all the teaching they could get, and learning to read from some simple Chinese books that Pollard had given them—there was no Miao literature in existence at that time. When their stores of oatmeal were nearly exhausted they regretfully set out for home, with the good wishes of everyone.

Before departing they assured Pollard that they were merely scouts who had come to see

The Coming of the Scouts

what truth there was in the rumours about the foreign teacher and his message. They declared that there were thousands of their fellow-tribesmen in the hills who were anxious to learn about Ie-su.

We must not blame Pollard that he was sceptical about this report; the ignorance and simplicity of the Miao were well-known. Most of them could not count further than twenty or thirty, and they could have no idea of what thousands meant. Little wonder, too, that the missionary who had toiled for years in south-west China and had only gathered a few Chinese and Nosu converts, was slow to believe that thousands of hillmen within a few days' journey were literally waiting to embrace the Gospel.

A few days later five more Miao filed shyly through the big gateway of the mission, slid their sacks of oatmeal to the ground, and asked for the teacher. Like the first party, they were accommodated in the empty schoolroom, and spent several days in intensive study of the Gospels in Chinese, under the tuition of Pollard and his staff. Their coming made Pollard think seriously of the story the first scouts had brought of the waiting thousands on the hills. When he saw thirteen more Miao march boldly through the big gates on the following day, he realised he must take the situation seriously. The unused schoolroom was now well filled with the eighteen Miao, struggling to read the simple Bible stories Pollard put into their hands, and with an appetite for Gospel teaching that could not be even partially appeased.

Sam Pollard of Yunnan

"Aren't you afraid of us?" Pollard asked them one day, impressed by the childlike trust with which these hillmen made themselves at home in the foreigners' schoolroom, placing themselves completely in his power when the big gates were shut for the night. He could not imagine Chinese country people, who despised the Miao, taking such risks with a foreigner of whom they stood in awe. In a flash Pollard got his answer.

"We heard the Chinese and the Nosu often talking about the yang-ren (the Chinese term for foreigners) and we were nervous when first coming to you. By and by, after seeing you, we found you were not yang-ren, but just like our own people. You are one family with us, only you have come from a long distance."

Pollard's heart leapt with delight at their claim to be of one family with him. That which to the Chinese would have been an insult was to the Christian missionary the greatest compliment that had been paid him in his life.

During that month eighty Miao passed through the mission house and went back to their homes in the hills. There was no gainsaying the spirit and persistence of these inquirers, the ambassadors of a great multitude. Every batch brought the same story—there were thousands waiting in their villages, as yet afraid to venture on the long and strange journey to the teacher in the city. Unlike the Chinese, who were full of curiosity about life in the white men's country, these Miao scouts had but one unvarying request, "Give

The Coming of the Scouts

us books and teach us about Jesus." They lived in the old schoolroom in the simple way in which they kept body and soul together on their journey. A little cold water was all they asked for. With this they could mix some of their oatmeal into a dough in their little wooden basins, and their only food was then ready for consumption.

Even at this point Pollard and his friends did not fully realise the situation that was facing them. They knew that within a hundred miles' radius of Chaotong there were at least five hundred Miao hamlets and villages. In them were crowded a people who had been landless and almost moneyless for generations, with no written language, no schools, and practically no intercourse with other peoples. Slaves of their Nosu masters or Chinese rulers, they worked unceasingly in return for the oatmeal that alone kept them alive. Without gods or idols, they were nevertheless in the grip of superstition, and victims of the two vices of drunkenness and immorality. Their houses were wretched hovels, and their only recreation and social life was found in the village clubs. In those clubs the younger people, married and unmarried, spent their evenings in a manner that was so immoral that the Miao who became Christians would never talk about it, and shunned these clubs as they would a plague.

After the first few raindrops came the deluge. No sooner had the first few parties of scouts returned to their villages with the story of their successful quest, than the number of inquirers increased ten, twenty, fifty, a hundredfold. A never-ending procession of Miao from the hills, each man carrying a sack of oatmeal on his back, passed through the streets of Chaotong, and through the big gateway into the mission courtyard. Very soon the mission-house became so chock-a-block with Miao that it resembled Hamelin town before the Pied Piper was called in; like the rats in the classic poem, the Miao swarmed everywhere. They overflowed from the schoolroom into the courtyard and invaded every room in the house—dining-room, study, kitchen, stable, and even the staircase. Sam could not move a step without stumbling over a Miao hard at work reading aloud from his little Chinese Testament. The man's face would light up with joy when he saw Pollard, and the missionary would be instantly buttonholed: "Please teacher, what is this word?" Even passing schoolboys were pounced upon to help in the task of learning to read. In vain did the missionaries try to restrict school hours or set definite boundaries for school work.

"Directly a door was opened," writes Pollard, "in they trooped with their books, begging to be taught. They began at five o'clock in the morning, and at one o'clock the next morning some of them were still reading. When I wanted a bit of quiet, I had to shut the big doors and retire to a lonely room at the back, where I was safe from attack as long as my three lines of defence held out. I can assure

The Coming of the Scouts

you it was a glorious but most disconcerting experience."

Week after week the Miao deluge went on without prospect of cessation. From sheer exhaustion Pollard would sigh with relief when a large company of the hillmen, finding their bags of oatmeal getting empty, marched out of the mission gate to return home. In a few hours, however, any hope of rest and quiet for the overworked missionaries disappeared, for fresh relays of eager learners marched in.

On one occasion Sam was persuaded by his wife to retire to his bedroom for the afternoon to rest, for he was obviously dog-tired. She was quite certain that she could secure a little quiet for him. He reluctantly agreed, and to safeguard him from any possible interruption she locked the door at the foot of the stairs and removed the key. Half an hour later she crept quietly upstairs to see if her husband were asleep, and was astounded to find the bedroom full of Miao sitting on the floor round the bed, reading their books under the guidance of the missionary, making the best of the opportunity of getting the teacher all to themselves without interruption. Finding the door to the stairs locked and the missionary nowhere to be seen, they had climbed up the outside balcony, through a window into one of the bedrooms, and searched until they had found him.

Chapter Nine. CHAMPION OF THE OPPRESSED.

"THE foreigners are teaching the Miao to rebel against us."

"They are giving the Miao poison to kill their landlords."

These and other wild rumours began to spread among the people of Chaotong as a result of the increasing number of Miao who flocked to the mission house. It was generally believed that under the plea of finding out about the Jesus-religion, the serfs were learning how to throw off the yoke of their Chinese masters. Always credulous, the Chinese solemnly believed stories that Pollard dropped magic water into the mouths of the ignorant Miao, and so enabled them to read Chinese characters at sight, and was able, by smoothing down their hair, to impart to them the power of remembering all he taught them.

The fact was that the Chinese bitterly resented any movement that would make for improvement in the lot of their serfs. The result was an outbreak of persecution against both the Miao and their Christian teachers. The first mutterings of the storm reached Pollard when he learned that three Miao, returning from Chaotong, had been captured by the Chinese and ordered to deliver up the poison that had been given them by the foreigners for their landlords. Converts were

Champion of the Oppressed

subjected to violent persecution on their return home.

Matters reached a climax through the action of the sub-prefect of Wei-ning Chow, in whose district thousands of the Miao lived. This official was very ignorant and quite unaffected by the new spirit that had been permeating Chinese life in many places since the Boxer rising. He solemnly believed all he was told about the great plots of the foreigners to drill the Miao, lead them to victory over both Chinese and Nosu, and hand over the land to the whites. He sent a report to the governor of the province, solemnly accusing the missionaries at Chaotong of fomenting rebellion.

Pollard found himself facing the most difficult and dangerous situation he had ever met. It looked as though the mass movement towards Christianity among the Miao would completely overwhelm the mission and involve them in nothing but disaster. He faced up to the situation in a big, courageous way. He would not turn his back on the Miao and deny them the light they were seeking. Nor would he let the whole work of the mission be stultified by the unfounded suspicions of the Chinese and Nosu. Above all, he must avoid the Government stepping in, for this would bring soldiers, pillage and robbery into the district on the plea of stamping out the persecution of the foreigners—and that would react in permanent hatred of Christians and missionaries. Thinking it all over, Pollard could only see one method though a hazardous one, of saving

Sam Pollard of Yunnan

the situation. He must go into the danger zone himself, not merely to trace the rumours to their source, but to conquer the enemy by friendliness.

He decided to go boldly to Wei-ning and beard the sub-prefect in his den. He would fain have waited a few weeks before starting, as it was the time of the after-rains, but he knew that delay might make a delicate situation worse. The journey proved that his fears were well-grounded. Half the distance had to be covered during the worst rainstorm Pollard had met for years—indeed, it was more like a cloudburst. He arrived at Wei-ning feeling and looking like a drowned rat, only to find that the sub-prefect was away visiting a higher official some days' journey distant. Fortunately, however, the two places were connected by telegraph, and Pollard succeeded in settling his business over the wire. A proclamation was drafted beginning, " Whereas we have repeatedly received Imperial Edicts commanding us to protect the Foreign men, etc." Now the courageous missionary was not in fear about the foreigners, but he was desperately anxious about his Miao converts, so he tactfully suggested that the words " Foreign men " should be altered to " Christians " and after some discussion this was agreed to.

His next move was to secure two official messengers to travel with him throughout the disturbed districts to make the proclamation known, and to secure the protection for the Miao that it provided.

Champion of the Oppressed

Again and again on this journey the people turned right around, and there was peace where before there had been suspicion and unrest. It was all very well for the mischief-makers to stir up hatred against an absent, unknown foreigner, but it was difficult for such an attitude to be maintained when that foreigner stood before them dressed as one of themselves, small enough to be knocked down by the weakest man amongst them, and telling a story with a good laugh at the end.

On that journey they visited many of the castles or baronial residences of feudal lords, and met with a varied reception, and had some dangerous episodes. The risks that Pollard ran as he quietly faced a hostile crowd in some of the markets, were none the less real because he made light of them. He writes:

"Our arrival at Dog Market was the signal for an ugly rush towards us. We stood up and faced this rush, and then to the hundreds of people we told our story as boldly and kindly as we could. After reading the Official Proclamation, and speaking as friendly as possible to everybody, we left, glad to get away from a noisy, dangerous crowd, which looked as ugly as crowds in a bad temper can look."

As has often proved the case, this campaign of persecution and calumny worked out for the good of the cause in several directions. Among other things it resulted in a missionary journey into a district hitherto unpenetrated by the Gospel. One evening found them outside the

Sam Pollard of Yunnan

castle of Ta-Kwan-chai, " The Fortress of the Great Ruler." Sending in their cards, the party waited anxiously for a response. A few minutes later a messenger came out, uttered the one word " Ching " (invited), and solemnly marched them in as the guests of the great ruler, An-yung-cher. After the meal, Pollard talked to An till midnight, telling him the Gospel story and pleading for religious liberty for his serfs. Next morning the great ruler promised that all the tenants in his sixty Miao villages should be free to do as they pleased with regard to Christianity. They left " The Fortress of the Great Ruler " next day, having made a real friend of An-yung-cher— an alliance which was to serve them in good stead later on.

Pollard returned to Chaotong in triumph, having saved the situation for both the mission and the evangelising of the Miao. As may be supposed, the stream of Miao who came to learn of the new religion tended to increase as the days went by and the situation improved. A thousand of these mountain men came in one day, when snow was on the ground and the cold on the hills they had crossed must have been painful in the extreme. Naturally the problem of accommodation became acute, for in no case had these men come for a few hours' visit. Sleeping wherever there was room to lie, they stayed until their declining store of oatmeal bade them begone.

At one time, Pollard said, you could always distinguish a Christian Miao from others on the

Champion of the Oppressed

highway. Christian recognised brother Christian not by drawing fishes in the dust or making the sign of the cross, but by saying grace before the wayside meal of oatmeal and water.

A most difficult problem was the lack of knowledge of the Miao language on the part of the missionaries, and the ceaseless demand for books. Anything that would tell them about Jesus met their demand. Pollard admits that he was caught napping in this respect, for although they had prayed for a revival, and had longed for a great spiritual harvest from their labours, they had never dreamed of their prayers and longings being answered in that manner. They had started with a big stock of large-type Christian books, but these were soon exhausted. The whole staff of the mission—foreign and native—were learning Miao as fast as they could, so as to preach and teach directly, but there was no Miao alphabet to make it possible to translate and print parts of the Gospels for the Miao to read for themselves. As a temporary expedient, Stephen Li helped Pollard to prepare a short account of the Bible story in easy Chinese verse, and this, when printed in booklet form, met the need for the time.

With the passing of winter, the crowd of Miao inquirers seemed likely to increase. As summer drew near, however, terrible dangers loomed ahead, and to these Pollard could not shut his eyes. Sanitary conditions and knowledge of hygiene are conspicuously absent in China, and the overcrowding of the mission-

Sam Pollard of Yunnan

house by such backward people as the Miao conjured up a host of terrifying dangers to the European mind. During the winter months the peril of fire had been always present, with sleeping crowds packed into rooms and corridors, and native lamps put down everywhere. But with the coming of summer the spectres of typhus, fever, diphtheria, smallpox, leprosy and syphilis began to haunt the more anxious members of the mission. What would happen in the hot and rainless summer months, with six hundred or so primitive people crowding into the mission house? The thought was enough to tax the faith of a missionary of even Pollard's calibre. He took those fears, real or imaginary, to the throne of grace and left them there.

Long before the dreaded heat of summer days arrived, two factors combined to provide a solution to this problem. In the first place some of their visitors desired that the thousands in the Miao villages who would never dare face the long journey to Chaotong, should hear the Gospel message. One day, greatly daring, they asked Pollard if it were possible for him to visit their villages. Without realising all that would result, he said " Yes, perhaps." Thinking it over quietly afterwards, he saw that a preaching tour among the Miao villages would show the possibilities of settled missionary work there. If that development were possible, it would solve the problems connected with the Miao invasion of the Chaotong mission-house.

The other fact was that An-yung-cher now

Champion of the Oppressed

came forward with an offer of a piece of land on his estates for a missionary settlement. This gave Pollard great delight for its own sake, for it was the direct result of the trouble he had taken to make friends with this landlord of sixty Miao villages, who had been persuaded to give his tenants full liberty in religious matters. Other members of the mission hailed it as a quick answer to their prayers, and a complete solution to the overcrowding problem.

It also seemed as though their Divine Leader had settled for them a vexed question of policy that had emerged through the Miao invasion of Chaotong. With mission work established on the hills, the work among the Chinese in the city could be carried on without let or hindrance. This was of great importance, in view of the awakening among the Chinese in the cities north of Chaotong, that in itself demanded the full attention of the missionary band.

At their annual meeting early in 1905, therefore, the whole position was reviewed, and after a long discussion, Pollard secured his freedom from the work at Chaotong, in order to devote his whole time to the Miao.

He set out at once on an itinerary among the Miao villages that would turn the tide of pilgrimage away from Chaotong. This would also take him into the territory of An-yung-cher, and enable him to find a site for his future home. Wherever he went he was recieved with tremendous enthusiasm, for the news that he was to be their own missionary had spread like wildfire among the hillmen. It was not so

Sam Pollard of Yunnan

easy, however, to find a site agreeable to An-yung-cher and suitable for Pollard's purpose. Although the landlord was sincere in his friendship, he had his own motives for stopping the trek of his tenants to Chaotong. He was very anxious that his people should not mix too much with the outside world, lest they should lose their simplicity and could not be ruled so easily in consequence. But he did not want to pay too high a price for this, so the negotiations for the site of Pollard's new mission-house proceeded very slowly.

In the end An-yung-cher gave the mission ten acres of land at Shih-men-K'an—" Stone Gateway "—a spot quite unknown to Pollard, who hurried off to survey it. At first sight he was very disappointed, for it occupied the broad breast of a hill where a great amount of levelling would be necessary before building operations could begin. Looking closer into things, however, he decided he might go farther and fare much worse. Stone Gateway was in the midst of a large number of Miao villages, and the hill consisted of smokeless coal that would provide enough fuel for a generation. In the end he accepted the offer, and the land was formally made over to the mission.

Chapter Ten   **WITHIN AN INCH OF DEATH.**

THERE was not much grass at Stone Gateway, but in any case Pollard was not the man to allow it to grow under his feet. The formal gift of the land for the mission was signed on the 30th of March, 1905, and on the 1st of April Pollard began to prepare the site. At first glance everything favoured the enterprise. He found plenty of good water, some excellent clay for brickmaking, and an abundance of stone for burning lime and for building. One drawback was a complete absence of any timber; a second, and more formidable one, was lack of money!

No funds were available from the Missionary Society for work among the Miao; Pollard himself had no means, and the people were poverty-stricken. Nevertheless it was part of his creed that difficulties are made to be got over, so he called the Christians of the district together, and explained the situation frankly to them. They responded nobly, and through a large number of small gifts it was possible to build a chapel seating three hundred and fifty people, or with standing room for seven hundred. The walls were of mud, with a thatch roof, and the total cost was only £25—but the most ornate cathedral could not have given the simple Miao more joy.

In Western eyes it looked more like a cattle

shelter built against the hillside than a church for Christian worship. The back wall of the chapel was the hillside itself, squared down a little. With a thatch of dried grass, and a back wall that gave endless trouble through damp, there was nothing much to boast about in the first Miao chapel—but it was soon hallowed by evidences of spiritual power.

The scenes that followed the opening of the Stone Gateway Chapel on the 14th of May almost beggar description. Between a thousand and fifteen hundred people assembled for the Sunday services, and how to get them into a building that would hold only seven hundred standing was a problem beyond the missionary or Stephen Li. In the end they held the service in four relays. Pollard has tried to portray the scene, but with a little imagination we can read much between the lines we have quoted below:

. . . .

To make room for the crowds we took the forms out, and then the married women came in first. If you wanted peace it was always wisest to let the women have the first turn, because so many of them brought babies, and babies are not patient unless they are asleep. When there are fifty or sixty babies in an audience of mothers, somehow or other eloquent or simple sermons do not make the desired impression. At any rate, those which I preached did not.

When the women went out the men came in,

Within an Inch of Death

and then the crush was greater. With a lot of good-tempered pushing and careful manœuvring, six hundred men could be arranged in the chapel. When later on I was joined by my splendid colleague, the Rev. H. Parsons, he managed these crowds with great tact and skill. Looking quietly over the six hundred, he would decide on the line of attack, and then give orders for another fifty men to be admitted. Those inside did not like that order, but the men outside, often waiting in the cold or even in the snow, heard it with joy. The extra fifty were pushed into position, and then I have known Mr. Parsons, after a short pause, order in another fifty. They were stowed away somewhere.

I expect my colleague used to play Rugby football, for I have seen him "scrum up" that crowd in real orthodox style. He was always in good form as centre forward working from the rear. You must see the crowd to understand what that means. The crush was tremendous. The men stood at attention, hands by the side. There the hands remained all the time, and it was a good thing there were no collars or studs or ties to get out of place and need re-arranging. All that kind of civilisation had no place in those chapel crowds.

The preacher stood on a table inside a small railed-in enclosure. This enclosure was, of course, full of people. The table was against the back wall, and so, in spite of unsteady legs, it did not fall over. From this table the crowd was managed and kept in order, and the service

Sam Pollard of Yunnan

was conducted. There was always plenty of singing, and when a well-known hymn was announced, the roar was tremendous. Prayers were many and short. Long prayers were cut short by everyone joining in a final "Amen" at a signal from the preacher. No person praying kept on after that "Amen."

How full of excitement those days were! The strain was very great, but the joy was greater.

* * * *

No sooner was the chapel completed than three large lean-to buildings were erected, one for the missionary, and the others for "boarders." They were built on the same principle as the chapel, three mud walls with a thatch roof, the whole leaning against the hillside. The cost of these buildings was nominal. Pollard humorously called his dwelling "The Wonderful £5 House." In appearance it must have looked it. To that five-pound house he brought his wife and family and a lady missionary. At each end a small section was partitioned off for the use of the ladies and children. The main room in the centre Pollard describes as "bedroom and dining-room, dispensary and book-room, dressing-room and strong room, pantry and larder, mothers' meeting room, preachers' training-class room, Society stewards' vestry, and poor man's lawyer office! Yes, and it was one thing more: it was the Love Room of Jesus, the Saviour of all who are in trouble and distress."

Within an Inch of Death

Having successfully checked the invasion of the work at Chaotong by the Miao, and firmly established a mission station for them in the heart of their own country, Pollard now faced the problem of gathering in the harvest of souls. The childlike simplicity of the Miao people, and their eager acceptance of the Gospel, resulted in wholesale requests for baptism. Some missionaries might have been carried away by the obvious success of their preaching and, quoting the precedent of Pentecost, have added to the Church thousands of souls in one day. Not so Pollard. Knowing the danger of superficiality, he exercised the utmost caution and self-restraint in dealing with the Miao converts. Only the most eager and promising of those who asked for baptism were formed into catechumen classes, and there subjected to rigorous examination and a course of training. Only the most satisfactory of these catechumens were selected for church membership. After that he felt he could not reasonably deny the privilege of Christian baptism to these people any longer, so on November 5th, 1905, one hundred and fifty converts were baptised and received into the first Miao Christian Church.

Two months later the first Sacrament for the baptised converts was held, one hundred and sixty-four partaking during a service that lasted three hours. In the evening eight hundred people were packed into the chapel, standing in serried ranks with arms at their sides so as to husband every inch of floor space.

Sam Pollard of Yunnan

The people sang the hymns with such heartiness that Pollard feared the building might fall through the sway of such a massed audience. At every service large numbers of people begged for baptism.

The experiences of those days were remarkable in many respects. There was a spontaneous outburst of signs and wonders such as occurred in the early Church, and are described in the Book of Acts. On their own initiative the Miao Christians went out in pairs preaching and teaching among the villages, "without scrip or purse," taking nothing but Chinese Gospels to sell. Cases of demon possession were not uncommon; some of the converts seemed to possess the "gift of tongues"; others were so certain of the immediate coming of Christ that they gave up their work in order to be ready for Him.

Throughout this revival and in-gathering Pollard was strangely moved. Often he was so nervous that it was only by strenuously gripping himself that he could retain control over his emotions. At critical times, such as the first baptisms and first communion service, he felt "a strong desire to sit down and have a good cry," so great was the joy of harvest.

Long before this Pollard's second furlough was due, but again and again he postponed it, for he could not tear himself away. He sent his wife and boys home to England in November 1906, promising to follow them as soon as possible. As a matter of fact it was

Within an Inch of Death

not till early in 1908 that he joined them in the homeland.

The settlement of Parsons at Stone Gateway now led Pollard to put into operation a plan he had long cherished, of opening out-stations among the Miao villages. This would not only make the work more compassable at Stone Gateway, but save some of their converts a walk of from thirty to seventy miles each way to attend worship. The first obstacle to be overcome was the opposition of the Nosu landlords, most of whom were opposed to Christian propaganda on the ground that it would sow the seeds of independence. In the end he obtained a piece of land in a village called Mi-ri-keo—Rice Ear Valley—for establishing the first of the out-stations of the Stone Gateway Mission. Later on another chapel was built twenty miles to the east called Halfway House, and another towards the south at Changhai-tsi called Long Sea.

After this Pollard secured the promise of a site for another chapel at Ta-ping-tsi—Great Level—about one hundred and ten li from Chaotong. He therefore travelled to Yongshan, a further eighty li, and arranged with the mandarin for a school-chapel to be built within his jurisdiction. Imagine Sam's surprise to hear two months later that the chapel was still unfinished, because the mandarin of Yongshan had so worked on the fears of the landlord that he refused to allow any trees to be felled for building, and had tried to dissuade the villagers from becoming Christians. Sam could

Sam Pollard of Yunnan

hardly believe the reports brought to him by his Miao friends. Not only was there a powerful enemy working against him, but the soft-tongued mandarin was a treacherous enemy. Chang, the village elder at Ta-ping-tsi, hated Christianity, and was determined to keep it out of his village. He had used his authority to rob the Christians of their harvest produce by imposing heavy fines, not merely beggaring them, but terrorising them completely. Going further, Chang had determined to kill Pollard himself. Going to the mandarin of Yongshan, he had accused the missionary of fomenting rebellion, and offered to get the foreigner out of the way if the mandarin would give him protection.

"The mandarin was half-inclined to consent, but he seemed afraid of what might happen afterwards," reported the Miao. "So in the end he told Chang to bring the foreigner to him, and he would deal with him."

The situation was a delicate one and full of danger. In that obscure region Pollard knew that the death of a foreigner could be invested in mystery, or made to appear as the result of a careless step on the mountain path, or the act of wandering brigands. Tired though he was, the brave-hearted little missionary decided that the boldest course, and the most dangerous, was probably the best. Going straight to the yamen, he walked boldly in, and fixing the mandarin with his big grey eyes, said: "I have come to deliver myself up to you."

Within an Inch of Death

Taken by suprise, and unable to meet the steady gaze of those steely grey eyes, the magistrate stammered that he did not understand; then he protested that he had not ordered the missionary's arrest. Adopting a tone of authority, Pollard declared that he knew the whole plot, and insisted on giving himself up in order to avoid bringing others into peril. The mandarin maintained that the story of the plot was an idle tale, but Sam refused to be convinced and soon became master of the situation. In order to give credence to his own argument, the mandarin had to suggest that the foreigner should sleep that night in the yamen, to ensure his safety. Pollard countered this by suggesting that the magistrate should make Chang sleep in the yamen, in order to keep a watch on the plotter's movements. Thoroughly alarmed, the mandarin not only promised him full protection, but sent four policemen to keep a watch on Chang.

Next morning the magistrate, with full state retinue, appeared at the door of the humble Miao house where Pollard had spent the night, to offer the missionary his protection and help. Sam insisted that the persecuted Miao should have their goods restored, and be protected from any futher oppression by Chang. The mandarin promised to carry out these requests, but he was obviously afraid of being too hard on Chang, fearing lest that rascal should give him away. The day ended with the magistrate giving a feast to Pollard, after issuing a proclamation protecting the Christians, and asking

Sam Pollard of Yunnan

the landlord to provide the trees required for building the chapel.

Elated by this success, Pollard spent the next day preaching to the people of Ta-ping-tsi, baptising converts and preparing to start a Christian Church. He learned that Chang had disappeared from the scene, vowing to get his revenge on the foreigner. Pollard laughed when these threats were reported to him, forgetting that a baffled enemy is often a most dangerous one. That night some Christian Miao from the neighbouring village of Ha-lee-mee came to report that their Nosu landlord was threatening them with massacre unless they gave up the Jesus-religion, and that some of the Chinese had sworn a solemn oath to murder the foreigner at the first opportunity.

It is possible that Pollard's success with the mandarin of Yongshan had made him over-confident, or less prudent than usual, for he decided to go to the village himself. He spent the next day at Ha-lee-mee in preaching the Gospel to the villagers, and encouraging the Christians to stand fast in the faith. Somewhat to his surprise, he was invited to spend the night in the house of a non-Christian Miao, who had been among his congregation. Pollard accepted the invitation, concluding that the man had been impressed by the message, and was anxious to hear more of it. Between nine and ten o'clock that night he heard the occasional firing of a gun, but his host assured him that this was being done to drive away a devil who had been causing the illness of a man in the

Within an Inch of Death

village. As this was a common practice, Pollard thought no more of the matter.

Soon after midnight he was awakened by the furious barking of many dogs. Through the chinks between the logs that formed the walls of the hut, flashes of light could be seen everywhere. Then came much shouting, and a second later the door was kicked open. The sight that met Pollard's gaze made his blood run cold. Outside was a band of fierce, savage, yelling men, brandishing torches and weapons. Recovering his sang-froid, Sam whispered to one of his men, " What does it all mean ? "

" Capture—murder ! " answered the Christian Miao, dully.

Determined to meet death bravely, the little missionary put on his Chinese gown and went boldly out to meet his fate, hoping thereby to give his friends a chance of escape.

The enemy at once closed round Pollard, shouting at him fiercely in wild excitement, and threatening him with spears, guns, swords and clubs.

Apparently the village was too public a place for doing the foreigner to death, for Sam was hustled away into the darkness, together with two of his Miao friends, who were being cruelly beaten as they went. Pollard wondered why he was spared this brutality, until he noticed that a big Chinaman, armed with a long executioner's sword, kept close to him and watched his every movement. This fierce-looking giant fascinated Sam terribly, as a serpent fascinates its prey as it pauses to strike.

Sam Pollard of Yunnan

In the tense moments that followed, the little missionary thought of his wife and children in England, and prayed desperately for a way of escape. Soon they reached the edge of a steep bank, below which could be heard the trickling of a stream of water.

At this point a big ruffian gave one of the Miao Christians such a smashing blow that the man stumbled, lost his balance, and rolled down the sloping bank into the water. This caused some confusion, and seizing his opportunity, Pollard suddenly dashed away into the blackness of the night. He was handicapped by knowing nothing of his whereabouts. Jumping down the bank at a venture, he ran for his life down the stream, hoping in the darkness to elude his pursuers. Forsaking their other prisoners at once, the whole party scattered with a hue and cry in search of the foreigner.

Pollard's dash for liberty was soon over. His pursuers knew every inch of the place, and in a few seconds he was surrounded on a sandbank in the midst of the stream. This time the enemy determined to take no more risks of their prey escaping. There was a mad rush at him, and Pollard realised that his attempt at flight had brought him to a spot well suited for the fell purpose of his foes.

The first to strike was a big man with a huge club. Helplessly Sam watched him swing it round. It landed with a crash on the prisoner's ribs, and down he went into the wet sand. Blow followed blow, until Pollard prayed that

Within an Inch of Death

the next moment would be his last. If only they would strike him in a vital place and end his torture!

At that critical moment came an unexpected interruption. Half-dazed by his injuries, the missionary afterwards remembered seeing a man clad in a white sheepskin jacket suddenly step out of the surrounding mob. Dully he wondered what the man was going to do. A second later the stranger in the sheepskin jacket knelt down by Pollard's side, put his arms round the stricken man and interposed his body between the assailants and their victim. There was a moment's pause at this sudden turn of events, and taking advantage of it the man in the sheepskin jacket yelled out; "No more beating! No more beating!"

In this strange way Pollard was snatched from the jaws of death. The dramatic act of the man in the sheepskin jacket made the ferocious assassins pause. Were they going too far? Their frenzy began to cool, and taking advantage of the change in the situation, the man told them boldly that they had gone far enough. After a whispered consultation that Pollard was too dazed to understand, the party picked up their helpless captive and carried him up the bank to a big walnut tree and ropes were sent for. With a sickening feeling, Pollard realised that death by violence had been averted, merely to be followed by a felon's end by a hangman's rope.

The unknown man in the sheepskin coat now stood by the missionary's side, and possibly

Sam Pollard of Yunnan

his attitude, backed by the victim's pleading, made his assailants change their plans. The order for the ropes was countermanded, and after a mockery of a trial, Pollard was ordered to leave the district.

"They declared that if I came again, they would kill me without hesitation," wrote Pollard afterwards. "If any action were taken against them for that night's work, they swore they would kill all the Miao in the village. My host was called up and told that if ever he received me again, he would be fined a hundred taels, several pigs, and fifty catties of gunpowder. The leaders informed me that they were not under the authority of the mandarins, and that they were determined to rule their own concerns and keep all foreigners out of the district."

In a state of absolute collapse, Pollard was carried back to the house of the Miao, more dead than alive.

Chapter Eleven
THE WORD OF THE LORD.

FOR two days Pollard lay at death's door in the house of a friendly Miao at Ha-lee-mee. On the third day Dr. Savin arrived from Chaotong, after travelling all night to the help of his colleague. Next morning the injured man was carried away on a litter, face downwards, because he was much too bruised to lie in any other position.

Tenderly he was borne to the hospital at Chaotong, and for some days his life hung in the balance. Every part of his body, except the head, was a mass of bruises. He had a wound in the lung just below the heart, showing that he had literally escaped death by an inch, and several ribs were broken or injured. The torn lung gave Dr. Savin intense anxiety for several days; then the wounded man took a turn for the better. He was ill for weeks afterwards, and it is doubtful whether his nervous system ever recovered from the shock of that terrible night.

To evade all responsibility for the attack, the Chinese Government posted proclamations in the district declaring that Pollard's wounding was the result of a quarrel between him and a Shan—one of the non-Chinese races. From Sam's report to the British Minister at Peking after convalescence, we get a glimpse behind

Sam Pollard of Yunnan

the veil that he systematically drew over his perils.

"Three times in twelve months bands of militia have come at night to the villages in which I have been staying, to murder me. I reported the first case to the Consul. He did nothing in the matter, although two houses were burnt down and much suffering was caused to the converts. . . . In the Yongshan district, during the last few weeks, one of the converts has been brutally murdered; others elsewhere have been cruelly tortured. Threats are still held out to murder me."

When after two months in hospital, Pollard began to walk about with the aid of a stick, his doctors urged him to settle up his affairs quickly, and take his furlough. His shattered nerves were proof of the soundness of this advice, yet he insisted on spending several months in placing the Miao mission on a sound basis, before he would consent to leave China. Then after tearful farewells at every place, Pollard turned away from the Miao and began the long journey home for his second furlough, reaching London in May, 1908.

For eighteen months he remained in England, journeying through the length and breadth of the land captivating audiences, large and small with his thrilling stories and passionate appeals for missionary service. In December 1909 he again bade his wife and boys farewell, and set out for China in the company of a new recruit, the Rev. W. H. Hudspeth. They travelled overland through Siberia to Shanghai, and then

The Word of the Lord

rode up to Yunnan Fu by the new French railway that had been completed during Pollard's furlough. It was thus possible for him to get back to his work five weeks after leaving England, whereas his earlier journeys had taken five months.

This revolution in the time and means of travel may be noted as an illustration of the changes taking place in China at this time. We have no space here to describe the revolution in 1911, whereby the Manchu dynasty came to a dramatic end, and China ceased to be a monarchy. The outward political change was but the climax to a crumbling of the old order that had been going on for many years. Rebellion and anti-foreign riots now made many parts of south-west China unsafe for missionaries, and although Pollard and his party reached Tungch'uan in safety, the mandarins refused to allow them to go any farther. It was many weeks before this ban was removed, and even then the missionaries had to travel towards Stone Gateway by a roundabout route. They visited Long Sea and Rice Ear Valley, and at both places found the work fairly maintained, considering the unsettled period through which those districts had passed. At last they reached Stone Gateway, where Pollard had a tremendous welcome.

In the autumn of 1911, he was able to put his hand to a piece of work that he had dreamed of for many years—the building of a training college for Miao teachers at Stone Gateway. Here we may note that the cost of this and of

Sam Pollard of Yunnan

much of Pollard's work among the Miao was made possible by grants from the Arthington Fund, established by Robert Arthington, a Leeds merchant, for opening up new mission fields.

One stipulation made by the Arthington trustees, when giving this support to Pollard's work, was that he should spend part of his time in translating the Scriptures into the native tongue. To this task he had been turning his attention for several years past. As none of the aborigines of China had a written language, he had been forced to invent one. From his knowledge of their primitive character he had discarded the Roman letter in favour of a simple script, that in Western eyes resembles a form of shorthand. When this script was completed, Pollard tried it out with great success. Largely phonetic, and therefore easily understood and remembered by the most ignorant, it has been described as an adaptation of Braille, Pitman's shorthand, and Roman signs.

Pollard now turned his attention to translating the four Gospels into the script, seeking help of the British and Foreign Bible Society in this formidable and costly undertaking. At first the Society's officers feared that this script was but a temporary expedient, and that a Romanised form of the language would eventually take its place. Missionary opinion was divided upon this point, and with characteristic energy and impatience Pollard declared that when a successful Romanised system had been

The Word of the Lord

invented and brought into general use, the problem might become acute, but meanwhile his people needed the Gospels in a readable form without any further delay.

In the end the society agreed to print the whole of the New Testament in the Miao script, a decision that filled Pollard with joy. With the aid of other missionaries and the best native teachers, he worked at the Miao New Testament whenever he could snatch the time for it from the ordinary routine. His journals give us many interesting and amusing illustrations of the difficulties that emerged as this enterprise went on.

" Yah-koh and I did the ninth and tenth of St. John. The story of the blind man was delightful. Yah-koh laughed heartily again and again at the way the man showed that he was more than a match for the people who bothered him. I wish I could tell this story as it appeared to Yah-koh.

" When translating the passage describing how Jesus took a child into His arms and used him as a text to teach the disciples from, my Miao assistant pressed me to add the word ' kissed ' in the translation. I said it was not there. He said ' It must be there : Jesus must have kissed the little one : He could not have helped it.' "

Pollard now succeeded in tearing himself away from this translation work in order to cross Yunnan to meet his wife at Haiphong. On the way he stopped at Ta-ping-tsi, near the spot where he had been beaten, to baptise

Sam Pollard of Yunnan

a large number of converts in the half-finished chapel. Prominent among them were the son and daughter of the headman at Ha-lee-mee who had betrayed him into the hands of his enemies when he had been beaten nearly to death. With great joy the missionary baptised all these people—he was getting his revenge in a way that pleased him greatly.

Pollard never forgot that journey to Haiphong. Wild rumours of revolution in China and of war between Turkey and Italy in Europe filled the air after he had left Yunnan Fu. He reached Haiphong in safety and had the satisfaction of being re-united with his wife on Chinese soil once more after many years.

They were now in the thick of the revolution. He returned to Yunnan Fu with Dymond in time to attend a great state function in celebration of the establishment of the first Chinese Republic.

Everywhere he saw signs of the new times. In the Temple of Hell the idols had been torn from their places and pounded into mud, which was being made into bricks by gangs of convicts. The great gaps in the temple where the idols had formerly stood impressed Pollard deeply, for they represented the loneliness of the people and the emptiness of their lives, until the religion of Jesus Christ was put in the place of the old idol-worship. Once more he sent home an eloquent and urgent appeal for the occupation of Yunnan Fu by the United Methodist Mission.

Pollard and his family started for Tungch'uan

The Word of the Lord

and Chaotong on April 1st and had a great welcome at every point. In spite of all the disturbances the work had developed in many directions during the absence of the missionaries. There was a friendliness and eagerness for Christianity among all classes that augured well for the future. Several new chapels had been opened by the Miao, and native preachers had kept the work going steadily forward.

Towards the end of that year the little missionary made an extensive and lengthy tour among the Miao villages on the hills, visiting his missions and preaching in the native chapels, big markets, and wherever crowded audiences could be gathered to hear the Gospel story. Pollard writes glowingly of this tour:

" I admitted new members nearly every day, and the total for the first round was about two hundred. The Harvest Festival at Rice Ear Valley was a crowded occasion. On the Sunday after at Stone Gateway thirteen new members were baptised. On the following Sunday I was at Heaven-Born Bridge for another Harvest Festival. I had to hold the service in the open air, and all the forms were occupied by candidates for baptism who had passed their examination. In the glorious sunshine, with a soft south wind blowing, I walked up and down the ranks, and one hundred and seventy-six times in succession I repeated the words so dear to an old missionary's heart —' I baptise thee in the name of the Father, Son and Holy Ghost.' It was a glorious occasion. . . . Fancy that for dark Yunnan!

Sam Pollard of Yunnan

We have nearly reached the thousand for the year, and shall apparently go beyond it before the March returns are made up."

In a large measure these words are an epitome of Pollard's work for the two years that followed. Travelling. preaching, guiding, teaching, he wore himself out in his Master's service among these primitive people, working hard all the while at completing his Miao New Testament. It was a stupendous task, apart from the burden of other work, and he began to fear lest his strength should fail before its completion. He had never been the same man physically since his narrow escape from death at Ha-lee-mee, and although his native assistants knew it not, he was working under a sense of a race with time.

The outbreak of the Great War in Europe in August 1914 had grave repercussions in Yunnan. The news reached Pollard and Hudspeth at a time when they were trying to keep pace with the large numbers of Miao who were asking for Christian baptism. Sam was appalled by the great moral tragedy, and felt deeply humiliated when he heard the simple Miao praying for the war to stop, and that the peoples of Europe might practise the law of Christ. That he was a far-sighted Christian statesman is clear from some of the letters he wrote to his eldest son in England.

" The Christians here are very anxious about the European War and ask us very puzzling questions. . . . I find no means of justifying the war to our own people, and own up that it

The Word of the Lord

is wrong. The diplomacy of our own and of other countries is based on heathen principles, and Christ does not rule among the rulers. Would to God that England would frame her foreign policy on Christian principles! It might mean crucifixion for a nation, but as surely as the cross of Christ is the ground of the world's hope, so the crucifixion of a nation might be followed by a resurrection which would transform everything."

Early in 1915 the mission doctor advised that Emma Pollard and her youngest son should be sent home. This verdict found Pollard undismayed, although he felt that his own health was in serious jeopardy.

"I do hope that my life will be spared for me to finish my translation of the New Testament," he writes in his journal.

Calmly this heroic man and wife discussed the coming separation.

"What will you do if anything happens to me?" asked Pollard, to which his wife replied by a laughing counter-question:

"What will you do if Ernest and I get torpedoed?"

"Ah," he said, "I shall return and finish out here."

While his wife was busy preparing for her return to the homeland, Pollard went off for another preaching tour among the villages. Forgetting for a time the horrors of the war, he thanked God and took courage from the number of baptisms being made. He reached home to find his wife had been ill again, and

Sam Pollard of Yunnan

that Dr. Savin was urging her to expedite the sea voyage.

"I urged Sam to face England and not to wait, but he was visionary, and would not consent to leave then," Mrs. Pollard wrote. "He felt I was used up for China. If the Committee had proffered some useful work at home, I used to feel that he would have taken it, for at times he was so tired that he would fain have hidden from the natives."

If the physical frame of the little missionary with the white, washed-out face was giving way under the strain of the work, his courage and spiritual vigour were unbroken.

"You and I are the only ones of the Old Guard left out here," he writes to Dymond at this time, "and how much longer we shall be here one does not know. Let us do our bit and be true to the highest spirit of our fathers, that we may keep our part of Christendom clean and pure, and win souls as fast as possible."

It may be that premonitions that the end was near came to Pollard at this time. The sense of urgency under which he finished translating the last of the New Testament books into Miao reminds us of the deathbed scene of the Venerable Bede. His Miao assistants began counting the chapters and verses that remained to be translated, until the moment came when, with exclamations of joy, they cried, "It is finished!"

A few weeks later typhoid broke out in the large boys' school at Stone Gateway. Always alive to the peril of epidemics in a land where

The Word of the Lord

sanitation and hygiene were unknown, Pollard had tried again and again to get proper medical supervision for the school. But instead of better conditions being possible, the order came from England for expenses to be cut down. He dismissed the Chinese servants in the school kitchens, and replaced them by Miao women, who came in daily to cook for the boys. It is believed that they brought the infection, for in spite of all precautions the dreaded disease appeared in the school. Hudspeth, who had been inoculated against it, volunteered to nurse the boys affected, and unfortunately he caught the fever.

Without hesitation, and worn out though he was, Pollard insisted on nursing his sick colleague. The battle was a fierce one, but in the end Hudspeth's sound constitution won, and the crisis was passed in safety. But alas, at this point his nurse took the infection, and was so enfeebled in body that everyone knew his struggle with typhoid would be a grim one. Emma Pollard, although under orders to go to England, cancelled her preparations in order to nurse her husband.

Dr. Savin, though very unwell, paid a flying visit from Chaotong and found the sufferer's condition gravely critical. The doctor, a brave missionary, was torn between two loyalties. His wife was ill in Chaotong and Pollard needed him at Stone Gateway. Without hesitation he decided to return to Chaotong to bring his wife back to Stone Gateway, so that he might give medical aid to both, as they equally needed

Sam Pollard of Yunnan

it. Hastening into the city, the doctor arranged for Pollard's old school-chum, Frank Dymond, to go to take charge of the work pending Hudspeth's recovery.

Pollard suffered in silence while his wife and old school-chum stood helplessly by. They could do little but pray for strength for the sufferer in his battle for life. His thoughts were still on his work, for once he roused himself to ask about a cheque that needed his signature, and on Sunday morning he remarked, "It is not time for service yet."

On two occasions he looked up into his wife's face and smiled, and once when Dymond entered the room, he greeted him in the old familiar way, "Well, old man?" On Wednesday, (the 16th of September, 1915) he sank into a state of coma, and on the following day the heroic missionary had passed on to his rest and reward.

His bereaved wife and sorrowing colleagues, even in that dark hour, could not feel that the situation was one of unrelieved tragedy. Sam Pollard had died as he had lived, for the sake of others. He gave his strength without stint to the service of the Miao, and possibly had contracted the fatal disease through his noble unselfishness in nursing Hudspeth.

His spiritual children—the Miao Christians—were overwhelmed with grief and troubled in spirit because their father and friend had been taken away from them. They vied with each other in showing their sorrow and reverence for his memory. Out of their poverty they

The Word of the Lord

insisted on bearing the full expenses of his burial.

The Chinese coffin they procured was too big to go into the house, so the old "£5 house" became the scene of his lying-in-state. Thousands came to show their grief and affection during those three days that he lay there. Seeing their devotion it was impossible to think that Sam Pollard was really dead. His spirit would live on and on in the hearts and lives of the thousands he had brought out of darkness into the light.

A site for his grave was chosen high up on the hillside overlooking the village, as though the Miao would live evermore under his protection. The day came when they carried him up the steep hillside through the maize fields, with twelve hundred mourners following. They tried to sing as they climbed, but the words were choked by sobs. In a beautiful spot among the young oak trees, and surrounded by the riotous beauty of the wild rhododendrons and azaleas, they laid his body to rest. Stumblingly and with great difficulty, Frank Dymond conducted the burial service over his chum at what he has since described as "the greatest funeral I have ever seen."

• • • •

The years that have followed Pollard's passing have seen a ghastly war and a tragic peace in Europe, and a period of revolution, civil war, and chaos in China. All missionary

Sam Pollard of Yunnan

work ceased for a time, but, in recent years, there has been a remarkable growth in the Christian Church among the Miao. All whose hearts are moved by the epic story of his heroic life will surely respond to the challenge of his spirit and memory. Our tributes to his work are but mockery if we do not take active steps to carry it on and extend it further. Chaotong, Stone Gateway and the Miao centres offer abundant scope to those who desire to carry on Pollard's work in the same noble and unselfish spirit. Especially is there a crying need for able experienced teachers. Emma Pollard, in a letter to the author of this book, makes a moving appeal for teachers for the Miao :

"The boys and girls want an experienced secondary school teacher very badly," she writes. "There are not in our ranks many *able* teachers. The Chinese, through long tradition, emphasise memory-training, and are inclined to stuff students with too many subjects. An English lady would take up mind training, so essential to these primitive people, who know so well their need, and who are waiting patiently for someone to wave the magician's wand, and give them their desire. Can you wave it ? The Miao need an educational representative so much, so much. An experienced lady teacher is a crying need."

Who will answer the call ?